THE
HYMNS
AND
BALLADS
OF
FRED PRATT GREEN

With Commentary by

BERNARD BRALEY

First published in 1982 by
Hope Publishing Company, Carol Stream, Illinois 60187, USA
and
Stainer & Bell Ltd, 82 High Road, London N2 9PW, England

Green, Fred Pratt
    The hymns and ballads of Fred Pratt Green.
    1. Hymns, English
    I. Title
    264'.2   BV459

ISBN 0-85249-612-5

Printed in Great Britain by Galliard (Printers) Ltd, Great Yarmouth

Contents

Foreword

Anyone who knows and loves the *Methodist Hymn-Book*—and I am among them—knows this strange thing about it: that it contains very few hymns by Methodists, save only the Wesleys themselves. Charles and John tower over it, of course, and who would be without them? Yet it remains true—or it has been true until 1969—that after the Wesleys the Methodist contribution to hymnody was astonishingly small. Certainly very few hymns at this time well known and written by a Methodist were printed between the death of John Wesley and the late nineteen-sixties.

During the last twenty years this has changed; it has been irreversibly changed by Fred Pratt Green. Indeed, 1969 will always be an important year in hymnody because it was that year which introduced him to the world-wide circle of friends that he now has. Before that he was known as a hymn-writer, I think, only to those who used the *School Hymn-Book of the Methodist Church*—and, of course, to his own private circle. But once 'Christ is the world's Light' had appeared in *Hymns and Songs*, far more of us knew that a door had opened: and we now know that it is one which as long as hymnody lasts nobody will be able to shut.

At this moment I don't doubt that people are busy here and there on doctoral dissertations examining Fred's work. I myself have had more than one student choose this subject for a college paper. This isn't the place to offer an extended critical study of what has become such a large body of hymnody. But this I will venture to say. It has long been my conviction about church music and hymnody, indeed about all liturgy, that it is, when it works properly, what comes naturally to people when they are at their best. It is not what comes naturally to experts, but to people: it is not what comes naturally to the careless or the wilfully ignorant, but to people as the Church sees them—at their best.

iv

Fred's hymns are exactly that. There is a deceptive naturalness about their diction. They make it look as if it's easy to write a good hymn. In true Gospel-fashion, they hide all the effort and wrestling and self-criticism that went into their making. They are never ostentatious or self-consciously clever. What is equally welcome in these days, they are never hectoring or raspingly censorious. Their centre is Christ and the hope of the Resurrection, which is where it ought to be.

Reading the kind of thing he writes I am reminded that in *The Oxford Dictionary of Quotations* (the first edition, anyhow) many lines of hymns are entered, but the editors found it impossible to resist printing the whole, except for one couplet, of 'God moves in a mysterious way'. That is as near a perfect piece of hymn-writing as anybody is likely to come by because in every stanza there is something which is both memorable and natural: not a forced phrase, not a syllable of self-advertisement; instead of leaving the reader saying how clever Cowper was, it leaves the reader saying, 'That's what I have been saying all my life'. 'Behind a frowning providence he hides a smiling face'; 'the clouds ye so much dread are big with mercy...'; 'God is his own interpreter'. The real hymn-writer can do this: Watts and the Wesleys could; Montgomery could; so could he who wrote 'Inscribed upon the Cross, we see in shining letters, "God is love"', and she who wrote 'Gazing thus, thy love we see: learn our sin while gazing thus'. This art is not dead. In these coming pages we shall read, 'sold once for silver; murdered here, our Brother', '...and did not Jesus sing a hymn that night?', and that which may be the greatest single moment in even Fred's hymns so far—'most of all, that love has found us...'. What a gift this is! And how generously it is shared in these pages!

There is absolutely no reason why hymns should not be poetry—or why hymn tunes should not be music. The kind of poetry that serves hymnody is produced by a writer with a sense of proportion—an instinct (though it is not liberated otherwise than by very close and searching work) for what will communicate the message with the greatest simplicity, and at the same time the needed incisiveness. Inferior writers pack too much in, use words imprecisely, grow impatient of metre and rhyme, and in a general way show that they are too big for their boots and too small for the task. What Fred knows is that a hymn cannot do what it is designed to do—it cannot *be* a hymn—until it has been not only admired but appropriated by its singers. A hymn isn't a hymn until some unpoetic person has made it his or her own: until singers don't mind who wrote it, but remember it. You might almost say that a hymn 'comes of age' when it becomes, not something the church provides for the worshipper, so much as something the worshipper has brought from his or her home and offered in church.

It is here that Fred has served us so well. But we can be more precise: he has not only given us much; he has liberated us. He has given hymn-writers back their nerve. No longer are we fumbling around to find anything written by a contemporary which isn't either second-rate or tiresomely trendy. All sorts of people are writing hymns—apart from the leaders whom he so generously mentions in his own preface. If they aren't always doing it with success or distinction, it is good news that people are doing it at all: and more than anybody else, Fred has been saying, 'You too can help the church to sing'.

Methodism ought to be proud and thankful that Fred is of its fellowship; and people of other churches may be, by the same token, envious. This book needs no commendation from me. All I can say is that I am proud, personally, of being able to call myself a friend of this historic contributor to a field of literature which means so much to me. I myself know hardly anything about hymn-writing—just enough, perhaps, to realize how almost impossible is the task which Fred has brought to such a distinguished level. But let nobody suggest that he has finished his work yet. The day after this book is published, he will come out with something that will be part of volume two, as fresh, welcome and necessary as ever. Bless you, Fred, for all you are doing for the Church, where it so much needs to be done.

Erik Routley
Princeton,
New Jersey,
1981

Introducing Fred Pratt Green

Born in 1903, Fred Pratt Green is truly a son of the twentieth century. He was born in the village of Roby, now part of the environs of Liverpool.

His father, Charles Green, born in Oswestry, and his mother, Hannah Greenwood, born in Ellesmere, came to Liverpool in the eighteen-eighties in search of work, married there, and eventually built up a successful leather manufacturing business. His own youthfulness in the latter part of life owes something perhaps to his being born of long-living stock. Both his parents lived to be over eighty-eight.

Fred was a late arrival, with his sister aged 14 and his brother aged 9 at the time of his birth. He was born into a Christian home which he describes as a place where religion was scrupulously observed but never made burdensome. His father, a Wesleyan Methodist and sometime Local Preacher, had resigned this office because he could not accept the Doctrine of Eternal Damnation. His mother was an Anglican and while living at Roby, there being no nearby Wesleyan chapel, the family worshipped at Childwell Parish Church. He attended Huyton High School.

Just before the First World War, the family moved to Wallasey and to worship at Claremount Road Wesleyan Church. At first he attended Wallasey Grammar School but in 1917 became a pupil at Rydal, the Methodist Public School at Colwyn Bay. Writing in 1981 to Rydal's present Headmaster (Mr Peter Watkinson) Fred notes, 'I was happy at Rydal, which is something not all old boys can say of their school'. The occasion of this correspondence was a commission to write a hymn for the 1985 Centenary in celebration of Rydal's founding. The final verse confirms Fred's active view that one is never too old to learn:

> You we praise, Creative Spirit;
> Come, in Christ, to set us free
> From the perils that beset us
> As we plan our life-to-be.
> You, the God of past and future,
> Source alike of love and power,
> Teach us all, for all are learners,
> How to use this present hour.

and he freely acknowledges his debt to Rydal's great headmaster, the Reverend A. J. Costain, a keen sportsman, for a school in which religion was sensibly taught; and to one particular master, Mr A. G. Watt, whose subjects were English and History.

Happy but undistinguished schooldays ended in 1920 with the early ambition to become an architect but Fred was content to spend four years in his father's leather manufacturing business, an experience which is retrospect he would certainly not have missed.

During the pastorate of the Reverend William Rushby at Claremount Road Wesleyan Church, Fred was guided to offer for the ministry. He was a successful candidate in 1924 and after a year in the Severn Valley Mission Circuit went to Didsbury Theological College, where he distinguished himself in everything but Greek and games. Here Fred began to develop literary interests, writing in 1927 a play, *Farley Goes Out* which was performed for a decade throughout British and Overseas Methodism.

On leaving college in 1928, Fred was sent to the Filey Circuit, as Chaplain to the newly established Methodist boarding school for girls, Hunmanby Hall, where he wrote his first hymn *God lit a Flame in Bethlehem* (**196**); and fell in love with the French mistress, Londoner Marjorie Dowsett, whom he married. In 1981 they celebrated their Golden Wedding Anniversary.

His ministry continued in the Otley Circuit (1931–1934) and in the Bradford (Manningham) Circuit (1934–1939). Two days before Britain was to be at war, he came to London in the Ilford Circuit, stationed at Gants Hill. Then, in 1944, he moved from East to North London, to the Finsbury Park Circuit living at Grange Park.

Fred Pratt Green devoted himself wholeheartedly to the work of the ministry, which give little opportunity for outside interests and little time for the development of his literary talents. But while at Grange Park, a chance pastoral visit to the father of one of his Sunday School scholars brought him into touch with Mr Fallon Webb, a man crippled with arthritis, whose consuming interest was poetry. The friendship was of vital importance in the development of Fred's talents as an author. Fallon Webb was a competent poet. Learning that his son's pastor had written the odd poem now and again, he suggested they should both write a poem and at their next meeting criticise each other's work. It was this willingness to please his friend which very quickly proved that Fred was a poet. These two friends kept up their poetry compact for nearly twenty years until Fallon's death.

Three collections of Fred's poems have been published: *This Unlikely Earth* (1952), *The Skating Parson* (1963), and (by Harry Chambers, Peterloo Poets, Upton Cross, Liskeard, Cornwall, England) *The Old Couple* (1976). Here is an example of Fred's poetry recalling his youth.

> We boys went to work by the river-ferry,
> The gangways steep when the tide was low,
>> Leaning on the wind,
>> Dodging the spray,
> With the lyver-bird golden in the sky,
> And the rubbish blown out of a boy's mind.
>
> We came home at night by the river-ferry,
> The gangways flat when the tide was high,
>> Staring at the serpents
>> Of light in the water,
> With the lyver-bird leaden in the sky,
> And the rubbish blown out of a boy's mind.
>
> On days when the fog foxed the river-ferry
> We rushed for the lift to the Low-level,
>> Swaying on a strap,
>> Mouthing a fag,
> With only the draught from a black tunnel
> To blow the rubbish out of a boy's mind.

Fred has contributed poems to many periodicals, including *The New Yorker* and *The Listener*. His work is represented in many anthologies, notably Philip Larkin's *Oxford Book of Twentieth Century English Verse*, the chosen poem being *The Old Couple* which has been widely anthologised.

On leaving Grange Park, the birthplace of his active work as a poet, Fred was appointed to the Superintendency of the Dome Mission, Brighton, where he ministered to one of the largest congregations in Great Britain. After five years at the seaside, he moved in 1952 to the southern outskirts of London, to the South Norwood Circuit, stationed at Shirley. In 1980, he wrote a hymn in celebration of the Golden Jubilee of this church, of which an adaptation for wider use is printed at **119**. Verse 2 of the original looks back to the beginning of the Shirley church in 1931:

> In times of growing tension,
> Of stubborn social ills,
> As London spread still closer
> To Shirley's gentle hills,
> God's servants built a church here
> To meet a people's needs
> Whose names we justly honour,
> Their foresight and their deeds.

In 1957, when the Methodist Church in Great Britain appointed separated chairmen, that is persons to oversee a district without also having the responsibility of a local pastorate, Fred was appointed to the then newly formed York and Hull District, living at York. Whilst his pastoral and administrative gifts were invaluable in this task, he was very happy to return in 1964 to the local ministry in the London (Sutton) Circuit as Superintendent, with pastoral charge of Sutton Trinity Church. When Fred completed his service there in 1969, the phrase 'retirement from the active work' ill describes the fruitful years which were to follow.

Towards the end of the Sutton ministry, Fred found himself invited to serve as a member of the Working Party entrusted by the Methodist Conference in Great Britain to prepare a supplement to the *Methodist Hymn-Book* which came to be called *Hymns and Songs*. Fred the poet was challenged by his co-members on this committee to become Fred the hymn-writer and help fill specific gaps in the book on which they were working.

One of the members of that Working Party was Mr John Wilson, Director of Music at Charterhouse from 1947–1965. Just as Fallon Webb played a crucial part in Fred's development as a poet, so John was crucial to his development as a hymn-writer. John's penetrating, yet constructive, criticism and encouragement as well as his specific requests for words for particular tunes, have played a major role in Fred's retirement career. His activities within the Hymn Society of Great Britain and Ireland and in the annual *Come and Sing* sessions at Westminster Abbey were significant in making Fred's work known to a circle well beyond his own denomination and country of birth. (See Hymn 1 for further information on this remarkable musician.)

The Reverend Doctor Erik Routley, the renowned hymnographer, was the second person to exercise a significant influence on Fred's hymn-writing. Erik was working on the International Hymnbook *Cantate Domino* for the World Council of Churches and soon discovered Fred's gift of writing paraphrases in English of hymns in other languages to fit tricky metres. Erik's decision to work in the United States also placed him in a situation to make Fred's work known on that side of the Atlantic. He seemed the natural person to whom to turn for a foreword to this book, and both Fred and the compiler are grateful to him for his ready response.

There are many others to whom Fred owes a debt as will be plain in the following pages but a special mention should be made here of the *Methodist Recorder* which published so much of his writing in its pages. He has also long been an active member of The Hymn Society of Great Britain and Ireland and was greatly honoured by his appointment as a Vice President.

This book is the detailed record of Fred's fruitful years as a hymn-writer. Its publication in anticipation of his eightieth year is the brainchild of two publishing friends: George Shorney, President of the Hope Publishing Company, which acts as publishers to the Hymn Society of America, came up with a proposal to publish these texts at the same time as Bernard Braley, Managing Director of Stainer & Bell, who has compiled this book, made a similar suggestion.

Fred and Bernard were thrown together with their joint appointment in 1977, by the Division of Education and Youth of the

Methodist Church in Great Britain, to edit the hymn-book for all-age worship, *Partners in Praise*, which has been published both in London and then later by the Abingdon Press in the United States. It was appropriate to so ecumenical a hymn-writer that the dedication service for this book was in the Roman Catholic Cathedral of Saint Peter and Saint Paul, Clifton, Bristol.

A series of scrapbooks which Fred has kept (coming up to thirty of them at the time of writing) present a unique record of his work in his retirement years and provide insights into the whole hymn-writing scene in an exciting period. It was the fascination of these scrapbooks that led the compiler to cull from their pages the stories behind many of the hymns as well as to print the texts. Within the pages of his scrapbooks, we meet Fred's friends and colleagues in a way which makes it natural to refer to many of them in this book by their Christian names.

Not all the texts in this book can be described strictly as hymns. Some retell stories and one or two are protest songs. The word we have chosen to describe these is 'ballad'. They are printed as Part III with cross-references to the hymns in Part I for border-line texts.

I am grateful to all those who have granted permission to reproduce copyright material in this book. It is hoped *The Hymns and Ballads of Fred Pratt Green* will not only prove valuable as a book of reference for compilers of hymn-books and as a book for those interested in hymn-writing, but also as a book of devotional material for the everyday reader.

Bernard Braley
London
December 1981

Speaking Personally

Why is it there are periods when few new hymns are written and other periods when so many are written that one talks of 'an explosion'—or to use Erik Routley's more decorous word 'a renaissance'—of hymn writing? Why should the first half of the twentieth century be comparatively barren and the 1960s and 1970s strikingly fertile? What drove Watts to write his new-style hymns, and open the way for Charles Wesley? Or what drove Fred Kaan to do the same in our time? The answer is the same in each case: need. Isaac Watts in the first half of the eighteenth century, and Fred Kaan in the middle of the twentieth, began to write hymns for their own congregations because they felt the need to revitalise worship through hymn singing by expressing Christian insights, old and new, in contemporary language. The time was opportune and the need was imperative.

It is instructive to compare the situation facing the compilers of the 1933 *Methodist Hymn-Book* with that facing the committee in 1981/1982 labouring to produce a new book acceptable to the Methodist Church in Great Britain. The earlier compilers had little new material. It was too early even for the two outstanding hymn writers of that barren period, Percy Dearmer and Canon Briggs, to be well represented. There are only three Percy Dearmer hymns in the 1933 book and only two hymns by Briggs. But the committee working on the new book has had so much new material that striking a balance is an acute problem: how much of the old should give way to how much of the new?

The new 'movement' as I shall call it, had its pioneers and heralds, notably Albert Bayly, whose hymn-writing goes back to the 1930s and who in 1981 is still active at eighty years of age. But it was the arrival of Sydney Carter on the scene, with *Lord of the Dance*, unlike anything English congregations had been asked to sing, which dramatically opened the way for experiment. The folk hymn was born, or perhaps we should say reborn, bearing medieval carols in mind. With the Beatles about, and the Beat Generation in the wings, youth took to Sydney Carter, and momentarily the guitar displaced the organ. On another front Geoffrey Beaumont and the Twentieth Century Church Light Music Group were asking questions about new kinds of music to traditional words.

Fred Kaan, writing his new words in Plymouth, was enough of a traditionalist to gain almost immediate recognition. Shaken up by Carter, we could settle down to Kaan. Our debt to him, and to Brian Wren, whose realistic hymn on Christian unity, *Lord Christ, the Father's mighty Son*, was published in 1967, is immense. These two names stand out, bright stars in a galaxy of new hymn-writers and song writers. Little books of new hymns and songs, unauthorised by the Establishment, and more substantial ones from Galliard (principally for the Protestants) and Mayhew-McCrimmon (principally for the Roman Catholics) broke through the defences. If I may use a political analogy, without political intention: when there's a confrontation of Left and Right, the Centre comes into its own. By this I mean that it is hymn writers like Fred Kaan and Brian Wren, and many others one could name, neither too revolutionary nor too traditionalist, who were likely to serve the Church in a time of confusion. I suppose, if I were honest, I should describe myself as somewhat right of centre!

It is always exciting to share in any movement which is effective in bringing about needed change. Most of the time, however, one is not conscious of involvement. As it becomes natural, second nature, to think in a new way, so it is with writing. If you have been used to addressing God as 'Thou', it is hard to say 'You' (as many of us have found when praying in public); but in time it is impossible to say 'Thou', for 'You' has become entirely natural to us. This, of course, is a small matter, but it illustrates how the new becomes acceptable. In the much more important realm of ideas, of insights, new concerns about the nature and mission of the Church, a new sensitivity to questions of race and sex, are no longer strange and debatable. It is unquestionably true that the new hymns, no longer new, have played an important part in helping the Church to relate to the modern world. This is what Fred Kaan has done for us in a unique way. In 1966 it wasn't easy to sing:

God is not remote in heaven
But on earth to share our shame;
Changing graph and mass and numbers
Into persons with a name.
Christ has shown, beyond statistics,
Human life with glory crowned;
By his timeless presence proving
People matter, people count!

Even rhyming 'crowned' with 'count' was daring (though Charles Wesley did that sort of thing!), and the secular feel of the hymn was disturbing. No one shudders now. The danger is always that having accepted disturbing truth we pack it away in moth-balls.

Since my name has been linked with those of Fred Kaan and Brian Wren, I feel under some obligation to speak the truth about myself. To begin with, I belong to Albert Bayly's generation, not to theirs. Though the winds of change have disturbed my roots a little, I have never felt uprooted. My generation may have doubted the Virgin Birth; it never doubted the existence of God. We may have argued the difference between 'deity' and 'divinity'; we never doubted the absolute authority and lordship of Christ. Many had turned away from fundamentalism; we were never tempted to dismiss the Incarnation as myth. We had reservations about the resurrection of the body; we never doubted in our personal survival after death. I am not saying that I have not shared in some of the agonisings of those who belong to a younger generation; I am explaining what I mean by being 'right of centre'.

I came to hymn writing after a twenty years apprenticeship as a poet, during which I was sometimes asked to write hymns and refused. Perhaps I looked upon hymn writing as an inferior art. Certainly few poets have qualified as hymn-writers, though some poems have qualified as hymns. In the end, late in life, when in fact I was on the edge of retirement from the active ministry of the Methodist Church, I agreed to try to write hymns for specific tunes and to fill 'gaps' in subject matter. I found it a fascinating assignment. I had no doubt at all that if, as a poet, I had complete liberty to choose my themes, my forms, and language, to please myself, now, as a hymn-writer I must become a servant of the Church, writing what was suitable to be sung in an act of worship. This led me to a method which some people find surprising. If I wrote a poem, I might submit it to an editor, probably expecting a rejection slip, and probably looking with some disfavour on suggested emendations of the text. A poet is sensitive on this score; a hymn-writer must not be. I have come to regard myself much as an architect does. He submits a plan, based on known needs, but is perfectly willing to adjust or start again if those who know best think his plan is unsatisfactory. Does the commissioning body always know best? Perhaps not. But they must be listened to with respect. The hymn-writer needs to be humbler than the poet! So, since I am mostly trying to meet a particular need, I submit a first draft, enter into dialogue, as the saying goes, and listen carefully to criticism, not always yielding, for the hymn-writer has his own brand of integrity, but seeking to offer something which the Church can use. This process can, at times, be frustrating; usually, it is rewarding.

I think what I have just written will explain the contents of this book. My editor, when he planned it, decided to add background information to each hymn, and in doing so gave away my secret. Few of my hymns were written, as poems are written, because of a restless urge to create; most were written to meet a stated need, even to fit a particular, and sometimes unrepeated, occasion. One result, I suppose, is range. I have enjoyed celebrating not only the great festivals of the Christian year, but such unlikely occasions as the centenaries of the Bells of St. Paul's and of Huddersfield Town Hall!

How does all this fit in with our conception of a poet, and no doubt of a hymn-writer, as inspired? Was Ellerton less inspired because he wrote *The day thou gavest, Lord, is ended* for a missionary meeting and on further reflection revised it? It is among my favourite hymns and is still able to move me. That magnificent last verse! How can it inspire *me* if Ellerton was not inspired? To me inspiration, the 'given' element in all art, is the mystery that lies behind all creativity and that essential part of creativity we call craftsmanship. So I decide not to wait to feel inspired but to get to work, and to do my best.

How much more one could say! Instead: my special thanks to Bernard Braley, of Stainer & Bell Ltd and to George Shorney, of the Hope Publishing Company of America, for conspiring to produce this book, to Allen Percival and Carol Wakefield, and to all others who have worked on it.

Fred Pratt Green
Norwich
December 1981

A HYMN FOR THE NINETEEN-EIGHTIES
written for
The International Hymnody Conference
Oxford, 1981

How can we sing the praise of Him
  Who is no longer He?
With bated breath we wait to know
  The sex of Deity.

Our Father is our Mother now,
  And Cousin too, no doubt.
Must worship wait for hymnodists
  To get things sorted out?

O rise not up, you men of God!
  The Church must learn to wait
Till Brotherhood is sisterised,
  And Mankind out-of-date.

O may the You-know-who forgive
  Our stunned ambivalence,
And in our sexist anguishings
  Preserve our common-sense.

I

GENERAL HYMNS

The majority of Fred's work appears in this section in approximate chronological order, though here and there a hymn is printed out of place for reasons of juxtaposition. Translations, Ballads, and some of Fred's very early work are shown separately later in the book. There is also a section of hymns for special occasions like the centenary of the opening of a church building or the celebration of the life of a particular saint.

1 The Church in the World

6.5.6.5.D.
(Trochaic)

When the Church of Jesus
Shuts its outer door,
Lest the roar of traffic
Drown the voice of prayer:
May our prayers, Lord, make us
Ten times more aware
That the world we banish
Is our Christian care.

If our hearts are lifted
Where devotion soars
High above this hungry
Suffering world of ours:
Lest our hymns should drug us
To forget its needs,
Forge our Christian worship
Into Christian deeds.

Lest the gifts we offer,
Money, talents, time,
Serve to salve our conscience
To our secret shame:
Lord, reprove, inspire us
By the way you give;
Teach us, dying Saviour,
How true Christians live.

When in 1968 Fred was Superintendent Minister with pastoral charge of Trinity Methodist Church in the London Borough of Sutton, he wrote this hymn for a Stewardship Renewal Campaign as the phrase *money, talents, time* indicates. This was the period when the Church was being criticised for its over-concern with its own life and its failure to be involved in the world's activities. Little did he think it was to mark the beginning of his hymn-writing career.

John Wilson asked questions about the last four lines of the draft and so led Fred to add a touch of encouragement in his revision. They first read:

> Let the world rebuke us
> By the way it gives;
> Teach us, dying Saviour,
> How a Christian lives!

Fred also felt the new version avoided the difficulty that the words 'Let the world rebuke us by the way it gives' contradicted the saying of Jesus, 'Not as the world gives, give I unto you'.

Having looked at many existing tunes, he thought PRINCETHORPE was the best but none really fitted the mood of the hymn, which a friend described as 'abrasive'. In the end, he wrote his own tune SUTTON TRINITY with the help of musician friends. This experience taught him the value of having a tune in mind when writing a hymn.

After initial publication in *Hymns and Songs* the hymn has been widely reproduced, with translations into Swedish in 1972, to SUTTON TRINITY. The Journal of the Hymn Society of America (*The Hymn*) printed it in 1970 with the misprint *war of traffic* for *roar of traffic*! The Episcopal Church of America set it to Vaughan Williams' KING'S WESTON which Fred likes. It has found its way into other books in the United States, Canada and Australia, and across many denominations, including the Church of the Brethren, Lutherans, Baptists, the Church of Scotland, Methodists and Anglicans.

The John Wilson who first queried the last four lines was born in 1905 at Bournville near Birmingham, and grew up in the tradition of Congregationalist hymns and worship. After two years at Manchester Grammar School he went on to Dulwich College, and then to Sidney Sussex College, Cambridge, taking an honours degree in Physics and (later) the Mus.B. degree. Having always had an instinct for music, he decided at the age of 23 to make it his profession, and did a 'crash course' at the Royal College of Music, studying with Thomas Fielden, Henry Ley, C. H. Kitson, R. Vaughan Williams, Gordon Jacob, and H. C. Colles, while living with his uncle Sir Walford Davies, then organist of St. George's Chapel, Windsor.

He became a music master at Tonbridge School and then at Charterhouse, where he was Director of Music from 1947 to 1965, after which he was on the teaching staff of the Royal College of Music until 1980.

In his early thirties he became a member of the Church of England, and in his early sixties, while organist of Guildford Methodist Church, he also joined the Methodist Church—it being possible to belong to both churches. So he has had first-hand experience of three different traditions of English hymnody.

He has had a prominent role, as co-editor and researcher, in the making of various hymnbooks, beginning with *The Clarendon Hymn Book* (O.U.P., 1936), followed by *Hymns for Church & School* (1964)—a successful development from the old *Public School Hymn Book*. Then came the Methodist supplement *Hymns & Songs* (1969), where on the committee he

3

began his lasting friendship with Fred Pratt Green. This has been followed by two small collections for the Royal School of Church Music, and an advisory part in *Broadcast Praise*, the 1981 supplement to *The BBC Hymn Book*.

For the past 15 years he has sought whenever possible to promote the cause of modern hymnody, notably through the annual *Come and Sing* sessions in Westminster Abbey, and through his work for The Hymn Society of Great Britain. He has contributed about a dozen hymn tunes to current books, together with a number of arrangements and descant versions.

Outside the field of hymnody his chief publication has been *Roger North on Music* (Novello, 1959), transcribing and editing the voluminous essays of one of the most delightful writers of the late seventeenth and early eighteenth centuries.

2 The Uniqueness of Christ

10 11.11.6.

Christ is the world's Light, he and none other;
Born in our darkness, he became our Brother.
If we have seen him, we have seen the Father:
Glory to God on high.

Christ is the world's Peace, he and none other;
No man can serve him and despise his brother.
Who else unites us, one in God the Father?
Glory to God on high.

Christ is the world's Life, he and none other;
Sold once for silver, murdered here, our Brother—
He who redeems us, reigns with God the Father:
Glory to God on high.

Give God the glory, God and none other;
Give God the glory, Spirit, Son and Father;
Give God the glory, God in Man my brother:
Glory to God on high.

The *Hymns and Songs* committee of the Methodist Church in Great Britain gave Fred the beautiful melody from *Paris Antiphoner* (*1681*) which Ralph Vaughan Williams had harmonised. CHRISTE SANCTORUM is set in most hymn books either to *Now God be with us for the night is falling* or *Father most holy, merciful and loving*. It called for the Sapphic verse form which, excellent in Latin, is not suitable to the English language owing to its feminine line endings:

> Christe, sanctorum decus angelor*um*
> Rector humani: generis et auct*or*
> Nobis aeternum tribue benign*us*
> Scandere regn*um*.

To overcome this technical problem, Fred found a way of fitting words to the tune, strengthening the weak endings by the effective device of repeating the final words of lines 1, 2 and 3 in each verse and adding an emphatic last line. The metre adopted is in fact 10.11.11.6. rather than the Sapphic 11.11.11.5.

The extent of the hymn's use is revealed by naming just a few of the books which feature it. Besides *Hymns and Songs* and *New Church Praise*, we find it in the *Canadian Hymn-Book*, the *Canadian Catholic Hymnal*, the *Australian Hymn-Book*, the Royal School of Church Music's *Hymns for Celebration*, the *Boys' Brigade Hymn-Book*, the Hymns Ancient and Modern supplement *More Hymns for Today*, the American *Ecumenical Praise* and *Hymns of Faith and Life*, the British Broadcasting Corporation's *Broadcast Praise*, and in translation published in various Scandinavian languages. The hymn was first used officially in its correct form at Vale Royal Methodist Church, Tunbridge Wells, Kent, at a Harvest Thanksgiving in September 1968; it was sung in Westminster Abbey by a choir from the Royal College of Music in 1971 and again in the Abbey as the only modern hymn in the service to inaugurate the union of the Congregational and Presbyterian Churches; and was included in a televised *Songs of Praise* in 1972 featuring six church choirs from a newly-formed ecumenical parish in Bromley, Kent. It also ended the dedication service for *Partners in Praise* in the Roman Catholic Cathedral in Bristol, with brass fanfares, in 1980.

It was translated for the International hymn-book *Cantate Domino* into the French of G. de Lioncourt. The German version needed a human triune of F. Karl Barth, S. Leonhardt and Otmar Schulz. By 1980, Friedrich Hofmann wanted to turn the trio into a quartet by suggesting the need of an additional German verse to declare Christ's coming again as King and Judge, and got conditional permission. Friedrich has since commented on the translation of the whole hymn into German at several conferences. In 1980, too, the thorny question of sexist language caught up with the hymn and the Episcopal Church of America pleaded that the climate in the States was such that, in deference to women's rights, changes must be made. Fred replied that, whilst he would allow all the changes asked, and was delighted by the

5

final one, he hoped they would not persist in altering 'brother'. The changes requested were:

> Verses 1, 2, 3, line 1: 'he' to 'Christ'.
> Verse 2, line 2: 'man' to 'one' and 'brother' to 'an other'.
> Verse 4, line 3: 'man' to 'Man'.

Besides CHRISTE SANCTORUM, the hymn has been set to CHRISTUS URUNKNAK, an Hungarian carol tune, which Thomas Lagrady arranged and Robert L. Sanders harmonised for the *Canadian Hymn-Book*. Fred notes that Erik Routley, world scholar in the field of hymnody, likes ISTE CONFESSOR. Erik, in his authoritative *An English Speaking Hymnal Guide* (1979) called it:

> ...perhaps the most immediately successful hymn of the recent wave of modern hymn-writing in Britain.

3 The Glorious Work of Christ

8.8.8.8.
(with optional
Alleluias)

Glorious the day when Christ was born
Alleluia! Alleluia! Alleluia!
To wear the crown that Caesars scorn,
Alleluia! Alleluia! Alleluia!
Whose life and death that love reveal
Alleluia! Alleluia! Alleluia!
Which all men need and need to feel:
Alleluia! Alleluia! Alleluia!

Glorious the day when Christ arose
The surest friend of all his foes;
Who for the sake of those he grieves
Transcends the world he never leaves;

Glorious the day of gospel grace
When Christ restores the fallen race,
When doubters kneel and waverers stand,
And faith achieves what reason planned;

Glorious the day when Christ fulfils
What man rejects yet feebly wills;
When that strong Light puts out the sun
And all is ended, all begun;

Fred has indicated the following possible changes to meet the sensitivity about sexist language in the United States:

Verse 1, line 4: 'we all' or 'mortals' for 'all men'
Verse 4, line 2: 'What self' for 'What man'

He wrote this in 1967 for the *Hymns and Songs* Working Party to ILFRACOMBE, a tune by a contemporary British composer John Gardner, which calls for three Alleluias after each line. In his first scrapbook, Fred notes how this repetition severely handicaps the author. Every line must express a sentiment to which *Alleluia!* is an appropriate response. He acknowledges a debt to Christopher Smart's poem *Song to David* for the repetition of 'Glorious' at the beginning of each verse. When considering this hymn for possible inclusion in *More Hymns for Today*, a member of the Board of Hymns Ancient and Modern wanted line 4 of verse 3 to read:

And faith achieves what God has planned.

Fred's point is different:

I want to suggest that the good the world desires can only be achieved through faith—and faith in a religious sense.

In *Hymns and Songs* TRURO is printed as an alternative tune with Alleluias omitted and this is now the more usual form in which it is used.

The *Loose-Leaf Book of the Episcopal Church in America* and the American Roman Catholic Hymn-Book *Worship II* both print it with the Schütz tune for PSALM 47, which has one set of three Alleluias at the end of each verse. *The Review and Expositor*, a United States Baptist Periodical, quotes the last verse as an example of contemporary apocalyptic writing. The hymn is also included in *New Church Praise* (United Reformed Church), *Ecumenical Praise*, and *Praise the Lord* (Roman Catholic) amongst other books.

7

4 A Hymn for Holy Week

All is ready for the Feast!
Every Jew is wondering how
God will liberate them now.

Pilate, fearful of revolt
He, at all costs, must avert,
Puts the Legion on alert.

Listen! Galilean crowds
Hail the Man from Nazareth,
Jesus, riding to his death.

What authority he wields!
With a whip of cords he clears
Temple courts of profiteers!

Watched by priests and pharisees,
All he says and all he does
Fans the hatred of his foes.

Now he gathers those he loves
In a room where bread and wine
Turn to sacrament and sign.

In that dark betrayal night,
Moved by hope, or fear or greed,
Judas sets about his deed.

Jesus in the olive grove,
Waiting for a traitor's kiss,
Rises free from bitterness.

As he wakes his comrades up,
Torches flicker in the glen:
Shadows turn to marching men.

In that dawn of blows and lies
Church and State conspire to kill,
Hang three rebels on a hill.

Innocent and guilty drown
In a flood of blood and sweat,
How much darker can it get?

How much darker must it be
For a God to see and care
That men perish in despair?

It is God himself who dies!
God in man shall set us free:
God as Man—and only he.

Let him claim us as his own,
We will serve as best we can
Such a God and such a Man!

What does our salvation cost?
Jesus, we shall never know
All you gave and all we owe.

The last verse is provided as a proper ending when selected verses are sung. The middle section *Jesus in the olive grove* began life as a poem around 1965, and was later printed in March 1967 by the *Methodist Recorder* with the tune TYHOLLAND suggested, the words being sung to this tune at Trinity Church, Sutton, during Fred's ministry there. John Wilson proposed J. Crüger's HEIL'GER GEIST as a better tune and it was sung at a Westminster Abbey *Come and Sing* session on 19th May, 1971 by Farringtons School Choir, with verses 3, 4 and 5 sung a fourth lower.

Then, when the *Partners in Praise* Working Party was searching for a hymn which took us through the events of Holy Week, Fred wrote verses 1 to 7. If this seems a marathon, its brevity is astonishing as an expression of the drama of the Passion narrative. By all means pause between the verses: but it is effective when sung throughout. Verse 15 does however give an opportunity for selection when this seems right.

The hymn is also printed in *Pocket Praise*, a words booklet issued for the British Council of Churches Youth Unit, for both singing and meditation.

5 Dialogue

Life has many rhythms, every heart its beat;
Everywhere we hear the sound of dancing feet.
Life is this world's secret: Lord of Life forgive
If we never asked you what it means to live.

Life is meant for loving, Lord, if this is true,
Why do millions suffer without help from you?
Some who fought injustice added wrong to wrong:
Can it be that love is stronger than the strong?

It was you who promised: *All who seek shall find.*
What we find lies deeper than our reach of mind;
What we found was you, Lord, you the God Above.
You had come as Victim to the world you love.

Life is meant for loving. Lord, if this is true,
Love of life and neighbour spring from love of you.
Give us your compassion: yours the name we bear;
Yours the only victory we would serve and share.

The *Hymns and Songs* Working Party wanted to include a song section of items in experimental style, and in particular the folk style popular with groups. Fred cites Sydney Carter's *Lord of the Dance* as the best known of these songs at the time. The tune for which the working party sought new words was Robin Sheldon's JONATHAN in *The Anglican Hymn-Book*.

A marginal note in Fred's first scrapbook reads:

> It is experimental in the sense that it *argues rather than states* a Christian view of life (hence *Dialogue*). I called it, to the amusement of some, my *Hymn for Hippies*, who were then much in the news!

It was written in 1967, and sung in Westminster Abbey in 1969 in the very first *Come and Sing* series by pupils of Priors Field School, Godalming to illustrate a lecture about *Hymns and Songs* by Cyril Taylor. Of a television broadcast from Maidstone, Kent, in 1974, Fred notes, rather sadly, that the congregation, perhaps insufficiently rehearsed, were unable to get the right rhythm. Lee Hastings Bristol, Jnr. (Princeton, USA) set the words in 1978.

Fred's nineteenth scrapbook contains this letter from Diana Phipp and the rest of the Seniors...

> Dear Mr Pratt Green,
> I hope you are well.
> I am one of the members of the seniors group at the West Wickham Methodist Church. We were wondering if you could tell us what these two lines mean from your hymn 'Life has many rhythms', the two lines are:
>
> *Some who fought injustice added wrong to wrong*
> *Can it be that love is stronger than the strong?*
>
> We want to know because we sing this song a lot as it is one of our favourite songs.
> Thank you very much.

If only all congregations would question the texts of hymns they don't understand....

This hymn is in many books including the Church of Scotland Supplement, *Songs for the Seventies*, the United Reformed *New Church Praise*, the Baptist Supplement *Praise for Today*, the Methodist Church Division of Social Responsibility's *One World Songs*, the Scripture Union's *Songs for Worship*, and an American Roman Catholic hymn-book.

6 A Prayer for Wholeness L.M.

O Christ, the Healer, we have come
To pray for health, to plead for friends.
How can we fail to be restored,
When reached by love that never ends?

From every ailment flesh endures
Our bodies clamour to be freed;
Yet in our hearts we would confess
That wholeness is our deepest need.

How strong, O Lord, are our desires,
How weak our knowledge of ourselves!
Release in us those healing truths
Unconscious pride resists or shelves.

In conflicts that destroy our health
We diagnose the world's disease;
Our common life declares our ills:
Is there no cure, O Christ, for these?

Grant that we all, made one in faith,
In your community may find
The wholeness that, enriching us,
Shall reach the whole of humankind.

At a late stage in their deliberations the Working Party on *Hymns and Songs* met during 1967 in residential retreat. They had decided to include J. R. Darbyshire's well-known hymn:

Life and health are in the name
Of Jesus Christ our Lord

But even this did not meet the whole need. It was felt there was a major sphere of healing (in which mental healing was the prior necessity) not covered by Darbyshire's writing.

So Fred spent most of the night—in bed—struggling with this theme and produced a first draft by the following morning. During discussion by the Working Party, Brian Frost, then Director of the Notting Hill (London) Ecumenical Centre suggested the line 'Unconscious pride resists or shelves' to end verse 3. This was accepted and Brian thinks that it is the only time the *unconscious* (in the Freudian sense) appears in a hymn. Fred has always disliked 'shelves' on literary grounds, but agrees it is psychologically exact.

The Rev. Gordon Harris, a minister of the United Reformed Church, who also practises as a Jungian psychotherapist, chose it for a broadcast service. It is used at the Ipswich St. Raphael Club for Handicapped Persons as their own St. Raphael hymn, and it has been published in the *Canadian Hymn-Book* and the *American Lutheran Hymnal* amongst other collections. The Lutherans omitted verse three, substituted 'recognise' for 'diagnose' and concluded with:

Shall reach and prosper humankind.

The original last line in many published versions, amended above to avoid sexist language is:

Shall reach, and shall enrich mankind.

Tunes which has been used include INVITATION, MELCOMBE and DISTRESS.

7 Prayer for Healing

Here, Master, in this quiet place,
Where anyone may kneel,
I also come to ask for grace,
Believing you can heal.

If pain of body, stress of mind,
Destroys my inward peace,
In prayer for others may I find
The secret of release.

If self upon its sickness feeds
And turns my life to gall,
Let me not brood upon my needs,
But simply tell you all.

You never said 'You ask too much'
To any troubled soul.
I long to feel your healing touch—
Will you not make me whole?

But if the thing I most desire
Is not your way for me,
May faith, when tested in the fire,
Prove its integrity.

Of all my prayers, may this be chief:
Till faith is fully grown,
Lord, disbelieve my unbelief,
And claim me as your own.

This hymn, written in 1974, was requested for the St. Barnabas Counselling
Centre, an ecumenical community centre for healing in Norwich. It is now

sung in healing services there and elsewhere. Erik Routley called this hymn 'a little gem' and John Wilson wrote:

> Your hymn is also one I should always be happy just to *read*— which is not in the least to cast doubt on its suitability for singing.

It was first sung, to ST. BERNARD, in St. Barnabas on 4th June 1974.

Other reflective tunes are ST. HUGH and another, in Fred's eighth scrapbook, BOSTON COURT by a Newcastle-upon-Tyne composer, Tom Bates. The text was included in Timothy Dudley-Smith's devotional book *Someone who Beckons*.

8 The Lord's Day   S.M.

The first day of the week
His own, in sad despair,
Could not believe for very joy
The risen Lord was there.

Obedient to his word,
They shared what Jesus gave,
And, one in him, in breaking bread
Knew what it cost to save.

Each day throughout the week
As on the Lord's own day,
They walked in newfound liberty
His true and living way.

So on this joyful day
From needless burdens freed,
We keep the feast he made for us
To fit our inmost need.

How soon we forge again
The fetters of our past:
As long as Jesus lives in us
So long our freedoms last.

Today his people meet,
Today his word is sown;
Lord Jesus, show us how to use
This day we call your own.

In 1967, the *Hymns and Songs* Committee needed a hymn about the Lord's Day which took into account its relationship with the Sabbath. When the American Lutheran Church came to consider it for their hymn-book, they asked for several emendations. Apart from changes to cover the American concern on sexist words, Fred thought their ideas for verses 3 and 4 were an improvement on the earlier text which read:

And each day of the week,
And on the Lord's own day,
They walked in Christian liberty
His new and living Way.

So on the Lord's own day,
From needless burdens freed,
We keep a Sabbath made for us
To fit our inmost need.

Possible tunes are: DAY OF PRAISE, ST. THOMAS (S.M.) and GARELOCHSIDE.

9 The Call to the Ministry   L.M.
Whom shall I send, and who will go for us? (Isaiah 6,8 RV)

Whom shall I send? our Maker cries:
And many, when they hear his voice,
Are sure where their vocation lies:
But many shrink from such a choice.

For who can serve a God so pure,
Or claim to speak in such a Name,
While doubt makes every step unsure,
And self confuses every aim?

And yet, believing he who calls
Knows what we are and still may be,
Our past defeats, our future falls,
We dare to answer: *Lord, send me!*

Those whom he calls he purifies,
And daily gives us strength to bend
Our thoughts, our skills, our energies,
And life itself to this one end.

This hymn was sparked off by a request from the Presbyterian Church in Canada in 1968 for a hymn which could be used in meetings challenging youth to consider the Christian ministry as a vocation. The version printed in *26 Hymns* was sung to GRENOBLE in Norwich Cathedral in December 1970.

10 The Caring Church L.M.

The Church of Christ in every age
Beset by change but Spirit led,
Must claim and test its heritage
And keep on rising from the dead.

Across the world, across the street,
The victims of injustice cry
For shelter and for bread to eat,
And never live until they die.

Then let the servant Church arise,
A caring Church that longs to be
A partner in Christ's sacrifice,
And clothed in Christ's humanity.

For he alone, whose blood was shed,
Can cure the fever in our blood,
And teach us how to share our bread
And feed the starving multitude.

We have no mission but to serve
In full obedience to our Lord:
To care for all, without reserve,
And spread his liberating Word.

This hymn was inspired by the theological emphasis of its time (1969). After publication in *26 Hymns* (1971) it was included in the Supplement prepared for the United Reformed Church (*New Church Praise*) in 1975. The American Lutherans wanted changes, omitted a verse and put the second verse last: this is the version above, which Fred came to prefer as definitive.

The Music Editors of the *American Lutheran Hymnal* (1978) chose WAREHAM, but Fred prefers HERONGATE.

11 Listen!

What the Spirit says to the Churches
Is what he said to a church of old:
You who have ears to hear me, listen!
O how I wish you were hot or cold!

What the Spirit says to the Churches
He said of old to a church his Bride:
You who have ears to hear me, listen!
You loved me once but your love has died!

What the Spirit says to the Churches
He said of old, who is First and Last:
You who have ears to hear me, listen!
In times of testing you hold me fast!

What the Spirit says to the Churches
Is what he said who lives evermore:
You who have ears to hear me, listen!
I set before you an Open Door!

This hymn, written in 1968 and revised in 1970, is based on the second and third chapters of Revelation. It was published in *26 Hymns* to a tune EMBER by David McCarthy. A somewhat easier tune PARKSTONE was written for it in 1980 by Michael Dawney.

It was first sung, most effectively, in Guildford Methodist Church in March 1972. It is a hymn in an unusual metre and is one of a very few texts available inspired by this passage in Revelation.

12 The Holy Spirit and the Church   6 6.6.6 6.6.

Let every Christian pray,
This day, and every day,
Come, Holy Spirit, come!
Was not the Church we love
Commissioned from above?
Come, Holy Spirit, come!

The Spirit brought to birth
The Church of Christ on earth
To seek and save the lost:
Never has he withdrawn,
Since that tremendous dawn,
His gifts at Pentecost.

Age after age, he strove
To teach her how to love:
Come, Holy Spirit, come!
Age after age, anew,
She proved the gospel true:
Come, Holy Spirit, come!

Only the Spirit's power
Can fit us for this hour:
Come, Holy Spirit, come!
Instruct, inspire, unite;
And make us see the light:
Come, Holy Spirit, come!

© 1971. For permission to reproduce this text, see page ii.

This hymn for Whit Sunday was written in 1970 at John Wilson's request to the late Sir John Dykes Bower's tune LUDGATE. It was sung by Farringtons School at a *Come and Sing* session at Westminster Abbey in 1971 and was first published in *26 Hymns*, with an additional verse placed fourth:

> New perils ring her round;
> Unsure, she loses ground,
> And fears the battle lost.
> Come, Spirit, come! revive,
> In her the faith, the drive,
> The joy of Pentecost!

The editors of *More Hymns for Today* wished the fourth verse to be omitted, believing we should not harp on these things and that it perhaps represented a temporary condition to the Church. This is surely a debate which will remain undecided with successive swings of the pendulum. *Broadcast Praise*, the Hymn-Book Supplement of the British Broadcasting Corporation, published in 1981, also omits the fourth verse.

This, Fred agrees, shall be the accepted text.

13 Hope Completes the Trilogy

8.6.8.6.D.
(D.C.M.)

> Though Love is greatest of the three,
> And Faith one step behind,
> It's Hope completes the trilogy,
> Lest Faith and Love be blind:
> For hopeless Love is blind with tears,
> And hopeless Faith with rage,
> But Hope has seen beyond our fears
> God's juster, kindlier age.

> God does not ask our faithful Love,
> Then leave us in despair,
> When life's misfortunes seem to prove
> There is no God to care:
> But gives us Hope to steady Faith,
> And in our grief restore
> Love's confidence that even death
> Is but an opening door.

20

God give us Hope, if Hope we lack
Of these three gifts to man,
That Faith may never turn its back
On all that Love began,
But strive against outrageous odds,
Our new destructive powers,
To build a world more truly God's,
And therefore truly ours.

This text was written for a competition sponsored by the Hymn Society of America in 1970 asking hymn writers to contribute new texts on *The Theology of Hope*. It was printed with six other new texts on this theme in 1971. The first verse has been slightly amended. A suggested tune is ST. MATTHEW.

14 The Gospel of Love

7.6.7.6.
(Trochaic)

Other gospel there is none
Than the one Christ gave us;
Love it is, and love alone,
Has the power to save us.

Love is everywhere the same,
Sacrifices, suffers;
Love it is that bears our shame,
Love is what God offers.

Love is anxious to atone,
Seeks for just decisions:
Love it is, and love alone,
Heals our deep divisions.

In God's Kingdom all are one,
When, in love, we share it:
What advances have been won
Through the Holy Spirit!

In this spirit we must strive
For the world's salvation,
Offering all we have to give
Without reservation.

This is a text Fred has wrestled with for some time. He calls it a revision of a
revision of a revision made in 1980. A suggested tune is EXCELSIOR.

15 A Hymn in Honour of the Holy and Undivided Trinity

Chorus
10.10.6.10.

Rejoice with us in God, the Trinity,
The Three for ever One, forever Three,
Fountain of Love, Giver of Unity!

We would rejoice again, and yet again,
That God reveals his truth to mortal men,
Unveils for all to see,
In what he is, what we ourselves may be.

Antiphon

22

How long and earnestly the Fathers strove
To frame in words a faith we cannot prove;
But O how dead our creeds
Unless they live in Christ-like aims and deeds!

So let us all, rejecting none, remove
Whatever thwarts a reconciling love,
All ills that still divide
The fold of Christ, and all the world beside.

Antiphon

Rejoice with us that we may yet achieve
What God himself has dared us to believe:
The many live as one,
Each loving each, as Father, Spirit, Son.

This hymn was written in 1970 at the request of John Wilson who wanted to introduce antiphonal signing at the Hymn Society's Conference of that year. It was duly sung at the Act of Praise to a setting by John he called TRINITAS, published in *26 Hymns* and later in the Royal School of Church Music's *Sixteen Hymns of Today*. The elaborate title of the hymn is a reminder that Norwich Cathedral, with which Fred has had close associations, is dedicated to the Holy and Undivided Trinity.

Hymns on the Trinity are rare. Erik Routley, in a sermon for Trinity Sunday in the *Expository Times* began by quoting verse 2 of this hymn, adding that it expresses what no other hymn on the Trinity manages to say.

The hymn has been published in *Ecumenical Praise* in the United States, set to a tune by the American composer Alec Wyton titled ROUTLEY.

16 Adam and Christ

8.6.8.6 6.

What Adam's disobedience cost,
Let holy scripture say:
Mankind estranged, an Eden lost,
And then a judgement day:
Each day a judgement day.

An Ark of Mercy rode the Flood;
But man, where waters swirled,
Rebuilt, impatient of the good,
Another fallen world:
An unrepentant world.

And now a Child is Adam's heir,
Is Adam's hope, and Lord.
Sing joyful carols everywhere
That Eden is restored:
In Jesus is restored.

Regained is Adam's blessedness;
The angels sheathe their swords.
In joyful carols all confess
The Kingdom is the Lord's:
The glory is the Lord's!

This text was written in 1971 at John Wilson's suggestion for singing at the reading of the Genesis passage during a Service of Lessons and Carols. John also suggested Jeremiah Clarke's melody HERMON which is arranged as a simple anthem by John in *Sixteen Hymns of Today*. This useful hymn is also included in the BBC Supplement *Broadcast Praise* and the second Hymns Ancient and Modern Supplement *More Hymns for Today*.

Verse 3 line 1 was originally 'A little Child . . .'. If there are sexist-language objections, Fred suggests:

Verse 1, line 3: 'Ourselves' for 'Mankind'
Verse 2, line 2: 'But we' for 'But man'
Verse 3, line 1: 'At last' for 'And now'

17 Advent Song

6 6 6.6 6.
and chorus.

Long ago, prophets knew
Christ would come, born a Jew,
Come to make all things new;
Bear his People's burden,
Freely love and pardon.
Ring, bells, ring, ring, ring!
Sing, choirs, sing, sing, sing!
When he comes,
When he comes,
Who will make him welcome?

God in time, God in man,
This is God's timeless plan:
He will come, as a man,
Born himself of woman,
God divinely human.
Chorus

Mary hail! Though afraid,
She believed, she obeyed.
In her womb, God is laid:
Till the time expected,
Nurtured and protected,
Chorus

Journey ends! Where afar
Bethlem shines, like a star,
Stable door stands ajar.
Unborn Son of Mary,
Saviour, do not tarry!

Ring, bells, ring, ring, ring!
Sing, choirs, sing, sing, sing!
Jesus comes!
Jesus comes!
We will make him welcome!

In 1970, John Wilson asked for an Advent Hymn to the melody from *Piae Cantiones 1582* included in *Songs of Praise* as THEODORIC (Gustav Holst's arrangement of the melody) to words of Percy Dearmer. Fred's hymn is printed alongside the Dearmer text *God is Love: his the care* in *Partners in Praise*. The same tune is set in *Pilgrim Praise* for a hymn by Fred's hymn-writing namesake, Fred Kaan, also writing for the Advent Season. This hymn features in several modern anthologies, including *English Praise*, the supplement to the *English Hymnal*. John Wilson included it in a group of hymns to be used as simple anthems (*Sixteen Hymns of Today*) published by the Royal School of Church Music.

In America, it is published in *Songs of Thanks and Praise*.

18 Midnight Carol

11 11.11 11.
(Anapaestic)

With all fellow Christians who gather tonight
We wait in the darkness to welcome the Light;
For dark is the world at the dead of the year,
And dark are our churches till he shall appear.

In secular cities, whose glare is not light,
The revellers snatch at the pleasures of night;
In silence and darkness, where drifting is deep,
The dutiful shepherd takes care of his sheep.

How many this Christmas look up at the light,
And, blinded by evil, see nothing but night;
How many dismiss, as a tale that is told,
The love of the Shepherd, the warmth of his fold.

Then join in our carols this cold Christmas Eve,
For great is our joy if we truly believe
That Jesus was born in the dead of this night
To help us to live as the Children of Light.

This carol, for the Midnight Mass or Holy Communion on Christmas Eve, was written for use in Thorpe Road Methodist Church, Norwich in December, 1971 and printed in the *Methodist Recorder* that year.

The folk tune A GALLERY CAROL—for which this text is written—will be found in the *Oxford Book of Carols*.

19 Lived A Man   8.7.8.7.

In that land which we call Holy,
From of old a land of strife,
Lived a Man whose birth was lowly:
Great our debt to that one life!

Where the Roman legions sweated,
In a world where might was right,
Lived a Man whose love defeated
Deadlier foes than soldiers fight.

Where a proud and subject nation
Learned to scorn each lesser breed,
Lived a Man whose true compassion
Knew no bounds of race or creed.

Where men studied to be righteous
Strict to keep each trivial ban,
Lived a Man who came to teach us
Love of God is love of man.

Where God's People long expected
God would reign, or God had lied,
Lived a Man they all rejected,
Lived the God they crucified.

This our faith: he lives for ever!
Love redeems, though it is slain!
This his Church's whole endeavour:
So to live that Christ may reign.

This hymn, to be sung to STUTTGART, was written in response to a request in 1969 for something on the life of Christ from the late Alan Dale, author of *New World* and *Winding Quest*, seeking hymns suitable for use in secondary schools, a project which in the end proved abortive.

It was first sung at Colchester Castle Methodist Church on the occasion of a gathering of members of the Methodist Church Music Society in the London North-East Methodist District. As well as appearing in *26 Hymns*, it was chosen for *Partners in Praise*.

20 Harvest Hymn   8.4.8.4.8 8 8.4.

For the fruits of his creation,
Thanks be to God;
For his gifts to every nation,
Thanks be to God;
For the ploughing, sowing, reaping,
Silent growth while we are sleeping,
Future needs in earth's ﹐safe-keeping,
Thanks be to God.

28

In the just reward of labour,
God's will is done;
In the help we give our neighbour,
God's will is done;
In our world-wide task of caring
For the hungry and despairing,
In the harvests we are sharing,
God's will is done.

For the harvests of his Spirit,
Thanks be to God;
For the good we all inherit,
Thanks be to God;
For the wonders that astound us,
For the truths that still confound us,
Most of all that love has found us,
Thanks be to God.

It is hard for even a very good tune to replace an established one. Francis Jackson's splendid tune EAST ACKLAM was written in 1957 for the hymn *God that madest earth and heaven*, as an alternative to the Welsh folksong AR HYD Y NOS. Some years later, at a conference of the Methodist Church Music Society, the composer played a recording of it, which made a great impression and led to a suggestion from John Wilson that Fred should give it a new text, preferably on a harvest theme where new hymns were badly needed.

Harvest Hymn appeared in the *Methodist Recorder* in August 1970. A footnote gave permission for the hymn to be used on application to Fred Pratt Green. In the next few weeks, requests flowed in from Thurso in the far North of Scotland to Camborne in Cornwall; from Gorleston in East Anglia to Rhyl in Wales; from the offshore islands of Man, Wight, Guernsey and Jersey; 125 in all. It has now found its way across the world and the denominations and into at least one other European language. Fred notes fourteen hymn-books on his list by the beginning of 1982. Amongst many occasions it has been sung in Westminster Abbey by Farringtons School Choir and at the Royal School of Church Music's St Nicholastide celebrations. *The Lutheran Book of Worship* (*1978*) used a tune by Emma Lou Diemer, SANTA BARBARA, and Austin Lovelace used the text for an anthem published by the Choristers' Guild of America.

21 The Stewardship of Earth 11.10.11.10.

God in his love for us lent us this planet,
Gave it a purpose in time and in space:
Small as a spark from the fire of creation,
Cradle of life and the home of our race.

Thanks be to God for its bounty and beauty,
Life that sustains us in body and mind:
Plenty for all, if we learn how to share it,
Riches undreamed of to fathom and find.

Long have our human wars ruined its harvest;
Long has earth bowed to the terror of force;
Long have we wasted what others have need of,
Poisoned the fountain of life at its source.

Earth is the Lord's: it is ours to enjoy it,
Ours, as his stewards, to farm and defend.
From its pollution, misuse, and destruction,
Good Lord deliver us, world without end!

The original version of this hymn won a place in *Sixteen Hymns on the Stewardship of the Environment* which was sponsored in the early seventies by the Hymn Society of America. This was clearly before the controversy on sexist language had gained steam for they happily printed:

Long have the wars of man ruined his harvest

On later American representations, Fred changed this to:

Long have our human wars ruined its harvest.

The original version contained the following additional verse, omitted above:

Casual despoilers, or high-priests of Mammon,
Selling the future for present rewards,
Careless of life and contemptuous of beauty:
Bid them remember: the Earth is the Lord's.

There are two other principal changes in the definitive version. Line 3 of verse 3 read:

Now we pollute it, in cynical silence ...

Line 3 of the last verse read:

Now from pollution, disease and damnation ...

The hymn was published in *Ecumenical Praise* to Austin Lovelace's ECOLOGY and in *Partners in Praise* to a new tune STEWARDSHIP composed by Valerie Ruddle, an active member of the Methodist Church Music Society, who runs a choir and orchestra at Sevenoaks Methodist Church. It has also been included in the hymn-book of the Reorganised Church of Jesus Christ of the Latter Day Saints, *Hymns of the Saints.* Other possible tunes are LIEBSTER IMMANUEL, LIME STREET and CONSERVATION.

22 Bread and Wine   6.4.6.
An Offertory Hymn

Here are the bread and wine
Of sacrifice,
Signs of the love divine.

Homely the bread we eat,
The wine we drink,
Harvest of vine and wheat.

Christ in the commonplace
Of bread and wine,
Offers himself, his grace.

31

This is my Body, he said,
This is my Blood,
Broken for you and shed.

Those who on him shall feed
Shall never die;
They shall have life indeed.

Come, then, O holy Guest,
And be the Host,
Yourself our Food and Feast.

This hymn to be sung when the bread and wine are brought to the table was written for a competition sponsored by the *Oxford Diocesan Magazine*. The tune ENDSLEIGH GARDENS was written by Fred's ministerial colleague, Francis Westbrook and published in *26 Hymns*.

Francis, a life-long friend, was born at Thornton Heath, Croydon, in 1904. He became the most influential Methodist musician of his time. Concert pianist and organist, conductor and composer, he was dedicated to the raising of musical standards in Methodism, chiefly through the Methodist Church Music Society. He died in 1975, all too soon after his appointment to the Williams School of Church Music, Harpenden, England.

23 Christian Marriage
6.6.6.6.8 8.

Joint-heirs of the grace of life. (1 Peter 3, 7 RV)

The grace of life is theirs
Who on this wedding day
Delight to make their vows
And for each other pray.
May they, O Lord, together prove
The lasting joy of Christian love.

Where love is, God abides:
And God shall surely bless
A home where trust and care
Give birth to happiness.
May they, O Lord, together prove
The lasting joy of such a love.

How slow to take offence
Love is! How quick to heal!
How ready in distress
To know how others feel!
May they, O Lord, together prove
The lasting joy of such a love.

And when time lays its hand
On all we hold most dear,
And life, by life consumed,
Fulfils its purpose here:
May we, O Lord, together prove
The lasting joy of Christian love.

The origin of this text is unusual in that it was not responding to a commission or a request. Rather, it arose because Fred wanted to write words for Lawes' PSALM 47 and felt the need for new hymns for marriage services. It was published in the *Methodist Recorder* in August 1970, in *26 Hymns* (1971) and later in *Hymns of Faith and Life* (Free Wesleyan Church in the United States) and in *The Marriage Service with Music* (Royal School of Church Music). It also found a place in *Brides' Magazine*. John Wilson's first choice of tune is emphatically John Ireland's popular LOVE UNKNOWN, to which it was sung in Westminster Abbey at a *Come and Sing* session in 1979. Another possibility is ST. GODRIC.

24 The Baptism of Jesus

7.6.7.6.D.

When Jesus came to Jordan
To be baptised by John,
He did not come for pardon,
But as his Father's Son.
He came to share repentance
With all who mourn their sins,
To speak the vital sentence
With which good news begins.

He came to share temptation,
Our utmost woe and loss,
For us and our salvation
To die upon the cross.
So when the Dove descended
On him, the Son of Man,
The hidden years had ended,
The age of grace began.

Come, Holy Spirit, aid us
To keep the vows we make,
This very day invade us,
And every bondage break.
Come, give our lives direction,
The gift we covet most:
To share the resurrection
That leads to Pentecost.

This hymn began life in 1973 at a time when Fred was having extensive correspondence with Dirk van Dissel, then an Anglican theological student at Trinity College, Melbourne, Australia. Dirk was concerned at the anticipated absence of liturgical office hymns in the *Australian Hymn-Book* then under discussion and in particular was seeking a hymn on the Baptism of

Jesus. The correspondence discussed several drafts with immense care for detail.

Ian Stratton, reviewing the final version of this text in The Hymn Society of Great Britain and Ireland's *Bulletin* (January 1981), writes of it:

> ...suitable for use at adult baptism...must be counted a triumph—laconic, scriptural, and with conscious echoes of the early Christian baptismal liturgies.

It appears in the form above in *More Hymns for Today*. One School of Theology, though, is unhappy about the fifth and sixth lines of verse 1:

> He came to share repentance
> With all who mourn their sins.

To meet these scruples, the hymn may be taken as five 4-line verses, with the last half of verse 1 above omitted.

Suggested tunes are CRÜGER or OFFERTORIUM or (for four-line verses) PASTOR.

25 Christian Baptism S.M.

Lord Jesus, once a child,
Saviour of young and old,
Receive this little child of ours
Into your flock and fold.

You drank the cup of life,
Its bitterness and bliss,
And loved us to the uttermost
For such a child as this.

So help us, Lord, to trust,
Through this baptismal rite,
Not in our own imperfect love,
But in your saving might.

Lord Jesus, for his/her sake,
Lend us your constant aid,
That he/she, when older, may rejoice
We kept the vows we made.

In 1971, Francis Westbrook asked Fred to write words for a tune by a retired music master who worshipped at Kingsway Hall, London. A five-verse hymn was the result. The original verse 4 has not stood the test of time but the first three verses have found a place in *New Church Praise* and the *Australian Hymn-Book*, whilst the version with four verses above appears in *Partners in Praise*. Although Fred is happy for the three-verse version to be used, he recommends inclusion of the last verse.

The hymn was originally entered for a competition sponsored by the *Oxford Diocesan Magazine* in which it was published. It is now usually sung to FRANCONIA.

26 Little Children, Welcome!   6.6.6.6.

Little children*, welcome!
Earth is yours to live in;
Arms of love protect you,
Little children*, welcome!

Little children*, welcome!
Jesus cares about you;
Jesus now enfolds you,
Little children*, welcome!

Little children*, welcome!
We, the Church of Jesus,
We will help your growing,
Little children*, welcome.

Little children*, welcome!
God will make you happy,
Jesus save and keep you,
Little children*, welcome!

* substitute 'brother' or 'sister' where appropriate.

At a conference of the Methodist Church Music Society in 1972, Joy Potts from Wesley Grove Methodist Church, St. Helier in Jersey asked for a hymn which could be sung by younger children at Baptism. Fred wrote the hymn that night. Ivor Jones (convener of the committee of the proposed new Methodist hymn-book planned for the mid-eighties) wrote a tune and with Francis Westbrook at the piano it illustrated Fred's session on *The Art and Craft of Hymn-writing*.

It was printed in the Methodist Recorder in February 1973 with Ivor Jones' tune LITTLE BROTHER. Several years later Valerie Ruddle wrote an alternative WELCOME.

Fred's sixth scrapbook contains a letter from one of the Junior Church children at Wesley Grove. Here it is, spelling mistakes and all:

On behalf of the Wesley Grove Junior Church, I would
like to thank you for the lovely words you wrote for
our family Service when we sung it with the help of
Mrs. Le Cornu to the babys of the Cradle role....

We enjoyed singing the third verse 'we the Church of
Jesus'. It is a lovely hymn and sounds quite affective
when Mr. Jones's tune is added. Thank you very much.
Yours sincerely,
Sonia Scott.

Notice Sonia's wisdom. The children are not the Church of tomorrow. They are now part of God's family. *We* the Church of Jesus!

27 The Church and the Kingdom 7 7.7 7.D.

Where Jesus Christ is, there is the Catholic Church. Irenaus

Where Christ is, his Church is there,
What a faith to hold and share!
Those who hold it must not part
Church and Kingdom in their heart.
They, their worship ended, know
In that world to which they go,
Though no bells invite to prayer:
Where Christ is, his Church is there.

Where Christ is, his Kingdom grows,
His the truth that overthrows
Every harsh and godless creed
Born of fear, or hate, or greed.
Some who never called him Lord
Speak his reconciling word:
His all love that overflows:
Where Christ is, his Kingdom grows.

Where Christ is, his Church is there,
What a faith to hold and share!
Those who hold it must not part
Church and Kingdom in their heart.
Taught by Christ, they count as his
All who share his sympathies:
Certain, when his work is done,
Church and Kingdom shall be one.

This is one of Fred's favourites which he regrets is so little used or selected for hymn-books. The tune ARFON is printed in *26 Hymns*. In 1981 Fred amended the original fifth and sixth lines of verse 3 on sexist language grounds. They formerly read:

Taught by Christ himself, they find
All are kin who serve mankind:

28 Praise Him!

8.7.8.7.D.
(Trochaic)

Lord, you do not need our praises:
Yet all beings must adore
You who are the world's Creator:
To believers, how much more!
You, the First Cause, you, our Father,
Who shall see you face to face?
Who shall say where human seeking
Reaches into realms of grace?

Lord, your unbelievers praise you
In their love of humankind:
For there's nothing worth achieving
Lies outside your loving mind.
So shall scientists acclaim you
Seeing cause where some see chance;
Trusting in their dark researches
That your universe makes sense.

Lord, accept your Church's praises
For your Son, whose name we bear;
For your Saints, whose pure compassion
Teaches all of us to care:
For the faithful, who find courage
To proclaim your saving word;
For all those who serve your kingdom
Without knowing Christ is Lord.

This hymn, written in 1971, has been slightly revised to avoid sexist language.
It was printed in the original form in the *Methodist Recorder* in 1973. David
McCarthy has written the unpublished tune STOKE ROCHFORD for it.
EVERTON and ADRIAN are also suggested.

29 A Mature Faith

8.7.8.7.8.7.
(Trochaic)

When our confidence is shaken
In beliefs we thought secure;
When the spirit in its sickness
Seeks but cannot find a cure:
God is active in the tensions
Of a faith not yet mature.

Solar systems, void of meaning,
Freeze the spirit into stone;
Always our researches lead us
To the ultimate Unknown:
Faith must die, or come full circle
To its source in God alone.

In the discipline of praying,
When its hardest to believe;
In the drudgery of caring,
When it's not enough to grieve:
Faith maturing, learns acceptance
Of the insights we receive.

God is love; and he redeems us
In the Christ we crucify:
This is God's eternal answer
To the world's eternal why;
May we in this faith maturing
Be content to live and die.

These words, evoked by David McCarthy's NEW MALDEN, are to be found in *26 Hymns* (1971). When Fred received a book *Faith and the Faith* by the Bishop of Leicester he was delighted to find two of his verses quoted there.

The hymn was sung at the Methodist Conference Festival of Praise in June 1971 and published later in *Praiseways*, a supplement issued by the Presbyterian Church of Canada, and in the family worship book *Partners in Praise*. An alternative tune is RHUDDLAN.

30 Feed the Minds

C.M.

Man cannot live on bread alone,
Said Christ, the Living Bread,
Who when he taught the multitude
Made sure that they were fed.

Shame on us if we lack the love
Christ has for humankind,
We neither meet the body's need,
Nor feed the starving mind.

Still hungry millions cry for aid,
A prey to those who preach
Persuasive gospels that enslave
The minds we fail to reach.

Make us, O Christ, the ministers
Of all you have to give,
Until at last the nations learn
The truths by which to live.

Then science shall be sacrament,
As love insists it should,
And all things secular conspire
To serve our greatest good.

This text was written for a *Feed the Minds* service in Guildford Cathedral,
England, in 1971 to the tune THIS ENDRIS NIGHT.

31 The Word Became Flesh

The Word is born this very night:
Hail, Mary, full of grace!
A hanging lantern sheds its light
On Joseph's anxious face.

The Word must come in human form,
In God's redemptive plan.
A Babe takes every heart by storm,
But who will heed the Man?

The Word is born this very night,
And humble is the place;
The world is dark, but hope is bright,
And sinners look for grace.

The Word has come to end the war
Which Adam first began.
O bless the Babe who sleeps on straw.
And listen to the Man!

This began in 1972 as a hymn with antiphons (*The Word became flesh and dwelt among us, and we beheld his glory* and *Gloria, Gloria*). Then it was printed without the antiphons in the *Methodist Recorder* in 1972 with the last line:

But hearken to the Man.

Writing on the Feast of Stephen, 1972, Methodist Minister Arthur Gregory enquired:

Should not Bethlehem and the Sermon on the Mount—the distinction between them having already been brought home in Stanzas 2 and 3—now stand together, in the closing 'ad hominem' appeal, without any hint of antithesis? If, as I hope, you agree, the poem when published (as it surely must be) in a definitive version will end thus:

O, bless the Babe who sleeps on straw
And hearken to the Man!

Fred took the point, altering 'hearken' to 'listen', which is how it appears in
Partners in Praise.

The tune there is YORK, but Fred would choose IN DER WIEGEN
from Corner's *Geistliche Gesangbuch* noting the arrangement by Elizabeth
Poston in the *Cambridge Hymnal* (No. 143), repeated in *The Penguin Book of
Christmas Carols* (No. 13).

32 The Mocking of Christ

Matthew 27, 29

8.6.8.6.D.
(D.C.M.)

To mock your reign, O dearest Lord,
They made a crown of thorns;
Set you with taunts along the road,
From which no one returns.
They did not know, as we do now,
How glorious is that crown:
That thorns would flower upon your brow,
Your sorrows heal our own.

In mock acclaim, O gracious Lord,
They snatched a purple cloak,
Your passion turned, for all they cared,
Into a soldier's joke.
They did not know, as we do now,
That though we merit blame,
You will your robe of mercy throw,
Around our naked shame.

A sceptered reed, O patient Lord,
They thrust into your hand,
And acted out their grim charade
To its appointed end.
They did not know, as we do now,
Though empires rise and fall
Your Kingdom shall not cease to grow
Till love embraces all.

In 1972, Francis Westbrook wrote:

> I am haunted by the almost unearthly beauty of Tallis's THIRD
> MODE MELODY. You will know it. It is set to some
> impossible words by Addison in the *English Hymnal.* . . . Can
> you try your hand at three verses? I want to write an Anthem on
> the tune. It seems to call for something virile yet wistful.

This hymn for Holy Week was the response. John Wilson did some research
on THIRD MODE MELODY ('The Third Tune') by Thomas Tallis in
Archbishop Parker's Psalter (*c.* 1567) and Fred adjusted his words to fit. The
result was published in *Sixteen Hymns of Today*.

In *More Hymns for Today*, Cyril Taylor combined two tunes, ST.
MARY for the first four lines and WIGTOWN for the second half of each
verse. This marriage of two tunes is an ingenious way of giving the lift needed
for the last four lines of each verse.

33 An Upper Room 9.8.9.8.

An Upper Room did our Lord prepare
For those he loved until the end:
And his disciples still gather there
To celebrate their Risen Friend.

A lasting gift Jesus gave his own:
To share his bread, his loving cup.
Whatever burdens may bow us down,
He by his Cross shall lift us up.

And after Supper he washed their feet
For service, too, is sacrament.
In him our joy shall be made complete—
Sent out to serve, as he was sent.

No end there is! We depart in peace,
He loves beyond the uttermost:
In every room in our Father's house
He will be there, as Lord and Host.

This hymn was written in 1973 in answer to John Wilson's request for a text to utilise the beautiful folksong O WALY WALY in the actual form in which Cecil Sharp had collected and published it—the metre being not a conventional Long Metre but a more subtle 9.8.9.8.

Together with John Wilson's setting of the melody it was published in *Hymns for Celebration*, the Royal School of Church Music's non-denominational supplement of hymns for Holy Communion, and it was sung at the Service of Thanksgiving for the life and work of John's wife, Mary, in September 1974.

Australian editors sought to change the text to a normal Long Metre, but agreed to accept Fred's pleading for the original. As well as the *Australian Hymn-Book* and an Australian book on *Holy Week* by E. J. Dwyer, the hymn has been published in the *Canadian Catholic Hymnal, Sixteen Hymns of Today, More Hymns for Today*, as well as in local books. Frequently used now at Holy Communion, the first two verses may be sung before, the last two verses after, the sharing of the bread and wine.

34 Our Christ is Risen

6.7.6.7.
and chorus

This joyful Eastertide,
What need is there for grieving?
Cast all your cares aside
And be not unbelieving:
Come, share our Easter joy
That death could not imprison,
Nor any power destroy
Our Christ, who is arisen!

No work for him is vain,
No faith in him mistaken,
For Easter makes it plain
His Kingdom is not shaken:
Chorus

Then put your trust in Christ,
In waking and in sleeping,
His grace on earth sufficed;
He'll never quit his keeping:
Chorus

There is a warning to hymn writers in mauve ink added some years later to Fred's first scrapbook:

Experience has shown I made a serious error by repeating the first line of the famous hymn—this has led to some confusion.

Fred refers of course to Canon Woodward's *Our Christ is risen*. In 1967, the Methodist Working Party on *Hymns and Songs* thought Canon Woodward's words were dated but wanted an Easter hymn to the Dutch Carol Melody VRUECHTEN.

I wonder if J. R. E. Crane, Steward at the Dalkeith Methodist Church in Barbados would expect to have found his letter preserved in the very first of Fred's numerous scrapbooks? It records the singing of this hymn at his Church on Easter Sunday, 1972.

The hymn is printed in the Australian Methodist Supplement *Sing a New Song*, the United Kingdom Baptist Supplement, *Praise for Today*, the *Revised Hymnal of the Southern Baptists* in the USA and in *Partners in Praise*, as well as in various local anthologies.

35 Christ Arisen

6.7.6.7.D.
(with refrain)

How rich at Eastertide
The harvest we are reaping:
For Christ, the Crucified,
Gives comfort to the weeping.
Saved by his bitter death,
With all our sins forgiven,
We learn to live by faith,
For now is Christ arisen, arisen, arisen, arisen.

As first-gifts hallow all,
If offered in thanksgiving,
So Christ has died for all,
The First of all the living.
Wherefore, the blessed dead,
Who else had vainly striven,
Are one with him, their Head,
For now is Christ arisen, arisen, arisen, arisen.

The Lord, who taught the way
Of dying and forsaking,
Shall bring us to that day
Of our complete awaking.
Then let no ill destroy
The hope we have of heaven:
Come, serve our God with joy,
For now is Christ arisen, arisen, arisen, arisen.

In October 1981, John Wilson at last received what he had long wanted—a literal translation of the Dutch text belonging to the tune VRUECHTEN.

Writing to Fred, he said:

> You will recall that the Woodward/FPG *This joyful Eastertide* makes half of each verse a refrain, which is too much, while the Dearmer (in *Songs of Praise*) *How great the harvest is*, has no refrain at all.

John asked for a version in which each verse ends with the line *For now is Christ arisen, arisen, arisen, arisen*, as in the Dutch original. This was the response based on the Dutch carol translation.

36 Easter Carol

5.5.5.4.

After darkness, light;
After winter, spring;
After dying, life:
Alleluia!

Take his body down;
Lay it in the tomb;
Love has overcome:
Alleluia!

Turn away in grief;
Turn away in faith;
Celebrate his death:
Alleluia!

Come whatever may,
God will have his way:
Welcome Easter Day!
Alleluia!

This text was originally written in 1972 for a cantata on *The Seven Words* by Francis Westbrook. One reason it never came to be published was that the music was thought too difficult. When the text was accepted for *Partners in*

Praise in 1978, the words were printed in the *Methodist Recorder* with tunes invited. Fred was particularly delighted with one of the dozen received, a tune by Ministerial colleague Brian Hoare, a staff member at Cliff College. This tune RIDGEWAY calls for the repetition of 'Alleluia!' in each verse. The second tune, BATHEASTON, came from a member of the working party on *Partners in Praise*, Ida Prins-Buttle, who had earlier served on the working party of a previous Youth Department publication, the *School Hymn-Book of the Methodist Church*. As an Easter carol, set to BATHEASTON, it also found a place in *The Galliard Book of Carols* (1980), an all-the-year collection of material from the fifteenth century to the present day.

37 For a Memorial Service   L.M.

How blest are they who trust in Christ
When we and those we love must part:
We yield them up, for go they must,
But do not lose them from our heart.

In ripened age, their harvest reaped,
Or gone from us in youth or prime,
In Christ they have eternal life,
Released from all the bonds of time.

In Christ, who tasted death for us,
We rise above our natural grief,
And witness to a stricken world
The strength and splendour of belief.

This hymn, including an additional verse, was first written and published in the *Methodist Recorder* (1972). It was submitted in 1976 to the Roman Catholic Commission on English in the Liturgy, accepted by them, and then rejected as theologically inadequate. In 1980, with the omission of a verse and one small change in text, it was one of the four (out of 457) entries accepted by

the Hymn Society of America searching for new texts on the Christian life.
Despite its title, it is suitable for general use.

The original Third Verse was:

> They journey on! While we must stay,
> Our work not done, our time unspent;
> What baffles us to them grows clear.
> In Christ the Truth they are content.

A later version of this original third verse has as its last two lines:

> May we, each day, rejoice in grace,
> Each day our stubborn sins repent.

Among recommended tunes are: SOLEMNIS HAEC FESTIVITAS
and ALSTONE.

38 For a Church Festival   8.7.8.7.3 3.7.

Great our joy as now we gather
Where the Master makes us one:
Where we worship God the Father
Through the Spirit of his Son.
All who search
For his Church
Find it where his will is done.

Precious is the tie that binds us
To our God when faith grows cold;
Precious all that now reminds us
He is still our safe stronghold.
Faithful love
Serves to prove
Here the shepherd has his fold.

May we learn from Christ's example
How to use this House of Prayer:
He who loved and cleansed his temple
Wants us all to worship there.
God the Son
Shuts out none:
In his Kingdom all may share.

Lord, inspire us with your vision
Of a world which must be won!
Glorious is the Church's mission,
Long endeavoured, scarce begun!
'Faithful now'—
This is how
God's eternal will is done!

This hymn was written at the request of John Wilson to Herbert Howells'
tune MICHAEL for the Anniversary at Guildford Methodist Church in
Surrey in 1972, but its use is not restricted to festivals.

39 Let the People Sing! 10.10.10.4.

When, in our music, God is glorified,
And adoration leaves no room for pride,
It is as though the whole creation cried:
Alleluia!

How often, making music, we have found
A new dimension in the world of sound,
As worship moved us to a more profound
Alleluia!

So has the Church, in liturgy and song,
In faith and love, through centuries of wrong,
Borne witness to the truth in every tongue:
Alleluia!

And did not Jesus sing a Psalm that night
When utmost evil strove against the Light?
Then let us sing, for whom he won the fight:
Alleluia!

Let every instrument be tuned for praise!
Let all rejoice who have a voice to raise!
And may God give us faith to sing always:
Alleluia!

This was written in 1972 for John Wilson who wanted a hymn for a Festival of Praise or Choir Anniversary to Stanford's tune ENGELBERG. John points out that the tune ENGELBERG should never be sung without the composer's special 'Amen', which contains the climax of the melody—the one-and-only top E.

Whilst it has been sung on many musical occasions in many countries, notably at a Three Choirs Festival service, it is included here under 'General Hymns' as it seems suitable for many worship occasions. It was sung in Bath Abbey to a tune MIRIAM by Ida Prins-Buttle and in the *The Lutheran Book of Worship* (*1978*) it is set to FREDERICKTOWN. There are already several other settings by American composers.

Originally the first line read 'When in man's music, God is glorified', the change to 'our' being made to meet sexist-language objections. Fred maintains that the loss of the juxtaposition of 'man' and 'God' somewhat weakens the line.

40 One in Christ

8.7.8.7.D.
(Trochaic)

One in Christ, we meet together,
Called by Christ himself apart;
He alone, our Lord and Brother,
Makes us one in mind and heart.
One in him, we each would offer
All we most sincerely prize,
Learning, when traditions differ,
What it is makes others wise.

52

One in Christ, may we, his Body,
Find in him our common creed;
As his people, be more ready
To respond to others' need.
His we are, who, found in fashion
As a man, content to serve,
Never narrowed his compassion,
Never asked what we deserve.

One in Christ, may we discover
How profound the truth we preach:
That in God the good is never
Something out of human reach.
Not by chance the world's creation,
Not by chance was life begun.
God is love: and our vocation
Is to love till love has won.

This hymn was written for a United Service at Guildford Cathedral in January 1973. The Bishop quoted from it in a brief farewell statement pending his translation to Salisbury. The tune used was ABBOT'S LEIGH. Fred made minor revisions in 1975 leading to the text printed above. An alternative choice of tune is BETHANY.

41 At Evening   5.5.5.4.5.5.4.

Now it is evening
Lights of the city
Bid us remember
Christ is our Light.
Many are lonely,
Who will be neighbour?
Where there is caring
Christ is our Light.

Now it is evening
Little ones sleeping
Bid us remember
Christ is our peace.
Some are neglected,
Who will be neighbour?
Where there is caring
Christ is our Peace.

Now it is evening
Food on the table
Bids us remember
Christ is our Life.
Many are hungry,
Who will be neighbour?
Where there is sharing
Christ is our Life.

Now it is evening
Here in our meeting
May we remember
Christ is our Friend.
Some may be strangers,
Who will be neighbour?
Where there's a welcome
Christ is our Friend.

A request in 1973 from an Over-Sixties Club for a hymn to be sung at Anniversary celebrations to BUNESSAN led to this text. Soon it was in the repertoire of an Over-Sixties Singing Group travelling in the Manchester area. None could foresee that, from this local request, the hymn was to travel even farther, for the Presbytery of Albany (The United Presbyterian Church in the United States) later sponsored a contest for new hymns that used sex-inclusive terminology. *At Evening* was placed first.

An alternative tune AVOND by Norwich organist, Stanley Fuller, was published in *A.D.Magazine*, the periodical of the United Presbyterian Church and the United Church of Christ in America.

42 A Song of Celebration

Sing, one and all, a song of celebration,
Of love's renewal, and of hope restored,
As custom yields to ferment of creation,
And we, his Church, obey our living Lord.

Rejoice that still his Spirit is descending
With challenges that faith cannot refuse:
And ask no longer what is worth defending,
But how to make effective God's good news.

We need not now take refuge in tradition,
Like those prepared to make a final stand,
But use it as a springboard of decision
To follow him whose Kingdom is at hand.

To follow him: to share his way of living;
To shape the future as, in him, we should;
To step across the frontiers of forgiving,
And bear the burdens of true brotherhood.

Creative Spirit, let your word be spoken!
Your stock of truth invigorates the mind;
Your miracles of grace shall be our token
That only God in Christ can save mankind.

This text began life as a commission of the organisers of the ecumenical London Festival of Worship *That's the Spirit* in 1973, which brought together a rich range of contributions from contemporary artists, writers and musicians, and included the first-ever open-air Communion Service in London's Trafalgar Square.

When *New Church Praise* was in course of preparation, the newly formed merger of Congregationalists and Presbyterians in Great Britain (The United Reformed Church) asked for alterations to make this hymn more general in its usefulness. The altered text was then set by David McCarthy, who called his tune CELEBRATION. It was included in *Songs of*

Celebration (Nairobi World Council of Churches Assembly), in the *Johannine Hymnal* (American Catholic Press), and set as an anthem by Lee Hastings Bristol, Jr. (Princeton, USA). (See also **43**.)

43 Live in Us!

15 15 15.6.
and Coda

All who worship God in Jesus, all who serve the Son of Man
In the Kingdom he prepared for us before the world began,
Are committed to his purpose in the things we do and plan.
Lord Jesus, live in us!

When the forces that divide us threaten all that God has made,
When it's easy to find reasons why the truth should be betrayed:
We who bear the name of Christian, we know who must be obeyed.
Lord Jesus, live in us!

It's his deeper revolution which redeems us when we fall;
It's his reconciling Spirit shall make comrades of us all;
It's the joy of God within us cries in answer to his call:
Lord Jesus, live in us!
Live in me!

This is a hymn which has grown from unexpected roots. It began life in response to a commission for the London Festival *That's the Spirit* (see **42**), for which the briefing was a little imprecise. In the end, Fred wrote the preceding hymn for that occasion. *Live in us* was chosen in its original version for *Praise for Today*, the Baptist Hymn-book Supplement, to VISION, the tune by Walford Davies in an arrangement by his nephew John Wilson. It was broadcast in this version from Sutton Coldfield Baptist Church in 1975 and from Manvers Street Baptist Church, Bath in 1976.

Fred's ninth scrapbook has a page headed, 'A Song or Hymn for Jakarta—a request from the British Council of Churches'. A note explains that The World Council of Churches Assembly in 1975 was moved from Jakarta to Nairobi for fear of Muslim-Christian trouble. A new brief led to some alterations (noted below) to produce the version printed above. The hymn became part of the Resource Kit, *Jesus Christ frees and unites* issued by the World Council of Churches. The hymn was later included in the hymn-book for all-age worship, *Partners in Praise*, although Fred did not feel the Music Editors' choice of DIVINUM MYSTERIUM from *Piae Cantiones*, 1582 was a really good fit for his text. The second edition commends the original tune VISION as an alternative.

In the original version Verse 1, line 3 read:

Know the purpose of his coming is the test of all we plan

Verse 2, lines 1 and 2 read:

As the need of man increases in a world that grows afraid
When the tempter finds a reason why the truth should be betrayed

Verse 3, line 1 read:

It's his deeper revolution that redeems us from the Fall.

44 Love, Joy and Peace

8.8.8.4.

The fruit of the Spirit is love, joy, peace.... (Galatians 5, 22 RV)

Of all the Spirit's gifts to me,
I pray that I may never cease
To take and treasure most these three:
Love, joy, and peace.

He shows me love is at the root
Of every gift sent from above,
Of every flower, of every fruit,
That God is love.

He shows me that if I possess
A love no evil can destroy,
However great is my distress,
Then this is joy.

Though what's ahead is mystery,
And life itself is ours on lease,
Each day the Spirit says to me:
Go forth in peace!

We go in peace—but made aware
That in a needy world like this
Our clearest purpose is to share
Love, joy, and peace.

This hymn was written for a United Women's Rally, in Croydon, London, and sung during the session on *The Fruits of the Spirit* addressed by the Metropolitan Anthony Bloom. It was broadcast in 1979 in The Hymn Society's Act of Praise.

The text is printed in *Broadcast Praise* and *More Hymns for Today*, to the tune RIPPONDEN, for which it was written.

45 The Mystery of Love   C.M.

Life has no mystery as great
As God, nor can it have.
You only, Father, can create
In us the faith we crave.

Mistaking mystery for myth
We throw our faith away.
O be the God we wrestle with
Until the break of day!

Awed by immensities of space
We worship you as Ground.
O be the Father we embrace
When we, the lost, are found.

So great the mystery of love
We half-believe it true.
O be the Crucified and prove
What love is and can do!

One of the small number of hymns Fred has written without receiving a
request! It was printed in the *Methodist Recorder* in August 1974 minus its
first line (duly corrected the following week).
Suggested tunes are ST. BOTOLPH or WIGTOWN.

46 God, Creator and Lawgiver
8.7.8.7.

Psalm 19

We look into your heavens and see
Your glory in creation:
There's not a sun or galaxy
But speaks our adoration.

We look into our wayward hearts:
How wisely you direct us!
Your law is where our justice starts:
Its clear commands protect us.

From mercy what have I to hide?
You hold me back from sinning.
O let me not be ruled by pride,
Where sin has its beginning.

That you approve my spoken word,
My thoughts and my behaviour,
Will be your servant's great reward,
My Sun, my Shield, my Saviour!

A last-minute difficulty over copyright led John Wilson to ask Fred if he

59

could provide, over a week-end, a paraphrase of Psalm 19 which would fit a 16th-century melody harmonised by G. H. Palmer entitled LINDEN TREE. A few weeks later, it was sung at The Hymn Society's 1974 Act of Praise in Wesley Chapel, York. It was reprinted in 1978 in *Sixteen Hymns of Today*.

47 Prayer

S.M.

Lord, now it's time to pray
My thoughts refuse to come,
Like children too absorbed in play
To turn their footsteps home;

And I confess with shame,
Their slowness to obey,
Knowing I am myself to blame:
They do not want to pray.

But when my thoughts are still,
Like children put to bed,
And silence teaches me to feel
How little need be said:

Then would I quietly sit,
To reach that point in prayer
When, Lord, the surest part of it
Is knowing you are there.

This personal devotional hymn or poem was written in 1974 to please himself. It was printed in the *Methodist Recorder* of January 1975 and may be spoken or sung to ST. BRIDE.

48 A Morning Hymn

6.7.6.7.6 6.

A new day bids us wake
To clear or cloudy weather,
And for each other's sake
Restores us to each other:
Remembering God, we say:
This is his world, his day.

As all life needs the sun,
Which never ceases giving,
Even when day is done
Its energy for living:
Forget God, though we may,
This is his world, his day.

Once more we rise to face
Another day's beginning,
To find in his free grace
Forgiveness for our sinning:
Resist God, though we may,
This is his world, his day.

So now, in solitude,
Or met in Christ together,
We praise our loving God
And pray for one another:
Believing, come what may
This is his world, his day.

In 1974, Erik Routley, commenting how good Fred was at working with
unusual metres, asked him to try his hand at writing a text for WAS IST,
DAS MICH BETRUBT, the 'poised and charming' tune from which 'that

wretched piece' FRANCONIA was derived. Fred wrote a text *The Grand Debate* with a final verse:

> Then join the Grand Debate
> But never cease to wonder
> At mysteries so great,
> And on their meaning ponder:
> And trust no final word
> Until you meet life's Lord.

This hymn was abandoned but its second verse became the second verse of *A Morning Hymn*, printed in the *Methodist Recorder* with an invitation to composers to submit tunes. Fred chose one by organist Ewart Knight though (reminding us that Fred has a good musical ear) querying one chord. BALESTRAND, inspired by the scenery of a Norwegian fjord, bejewelled in sunshine and snow, was printed and also sung at Teddington Methodist Church in November 1975.

The third verse of the new hymn was amended to the text above in 1976, having previously read:

> Each day we must renew
> This journey we are taking,
> And summon into view
> The future of our making!
> Forget God though we may,
> This is his world, his day.

49 A Plea for Christian Unity   6 6.4.6 6 6.4.

> What shall our greeting be:
> Sign of our unity?
> JESUS IS LORD!
> May we no more defend
> Barriers he died to end:
> Give me your hand, my friend:
> One Church, One Lord!

What is our mission here?
He makes his purpose clear:
One world, one Lord!
Spirit of truth descend,
All our confusions end:
Give me your hand, my friend:
JESUS IS LORD!

He comes to save us now:
To serve him is to know
Life's true reward.
May he our lives amend,
All our betrayals end:
Give me your hand, my friend:
JESUS IS LORD!

This hymn was the winning entry in a competition for ecumenical hymns sponsored in 1974 by Queen's College, Birmingham, England. WATCH-MAN was the tune suggested. Believing that a tune well-known to all denominations would be preferable, Fred later made minor changes so that the text fitted MOSCOW. When the Methodist Conference visited Bradford it was sung in the Cathedral there. Then in 1981 when the Conference visited Norwich, where Fred has made his home in busy retirement, it was sung again at an ecumenical service in Norwich Cathedral when some members of the congregation were moved spontaneously to shake hands.

50 This is the Night
10 10. 10 10. (Dactylic)
with Gloria (which may be omitted)

This is the night of his coming to earth:
Christ in the darkness is waiting his birth.
All is now ready, and each in their place,
Planets and people, this moment of grace:
Gloria!

This is the hour when a Mother must wait,
Wait until labour comes, early or late:
This is the moment the Babe in her womb
Knocks on the door of a carpenter's home.
Gloria!

This is the hour when we sinners despair:
This is the hour when the angels declare
Peace upon earth to all men of goodwill:
Shepherds see glory on Bethlehem's hill.
Gloria!

This is the night: let a trumpet be blown!
Never again shall love wear such a crown!
This is the hour when our souls find release:
Welcome to him who has come to make peace!
Gloria!

This text was written in 1974 to fit an old Hebrew melody that Ida Prins-Buttle
heard while travelling by bus from Jerusalem to Beer-Sheba. Ida, a veteran
world traveller, has made her voice heard in Methodism on many subjects
and has been a leading member of the Methodist Church Music Society. Her
tune EMMANUEL was sung by a choir of members of Women's Institutes
from all over Avon in Wells Cathedral at Christmas 1974, and was later
published as an anthem in the *Bourne Series* by the Williams School of
Church Music. It has also been sung in Bath Abbey, Bristol Cathedral and
many parts of Scotland, and in America by the choir of Springfield State
University, Missouri. With the Gloria omitted *This is the Night* can be sung
to QUEDLINBURG.

51 In Honour of the Virgin Mary   7.6.7.6.8.7.3.5.3.

Never was a day so bright,
Never maid so gentle;
Brighter than the brightest light
Shone the Lord's archangel.
Lady, you tremble at the news!
Tell us you will not refuse
To carry
Our little Lord of Love
And Glory.

Soon a sword shall pierce your heart,
Sadden your tomorrows;
All too soon you too must start
Up the Hill of Sorrows.
Lady, they will respect your grief,
When in darkness past belief
You tarry,
Bearing the cross that love
Must carry.

Wear the crown upon your brow
You alone are wearing,
Mother of all mothers now:
In his triumph sharing.
Lady, you were his home on earth:
Now your Son must come to birth
Within us,
By nothing else than love
To win us.

Fred wrote this hymn before breakfast one morning in 1974 in response to a
request for a hymn about the Virgin Mary which non-Roman Catholics could
sing to Francis Duffy's enchanting tune TROCHRAGUE in the Roman

Catholic Hymn-Book *Praise the Lord*, where it is set to the medieval hymn to Mary *Of one that is so fair and bright*. John Wilson, who commissioned it, raised some queries on the text, especially about line 5 in verse 2, which was influenced by Charles Peguy's *Passion of Our Lady*, but Fred reports he completely convinced John and the line stayed.

The version above is as printed in the Royal School of Church Music's *Sixteen Hymns of Today*. The original had the Latin 'Mater honorata' and 'Felix fecundata' for lines 2 and 4 of the final verse.

52 In Celebration of Saints

10 10. 11 11. or
55.55.65.65.
(Anapaestic)

Rejoice in God's saints, today and all days!
A world without saints forgets how to praise.
Their faith in acquiring the habit of prayer,
Their depth of adoring, Lord, help us to share.

Some march with events to turn them God's way;
Some need to withdraw, the better to pray;
Some carry the gospel through fire and through flood:
Our world is their parish: their purpose is God.

Rejoice in those saints, unpraised and unknown,
Who bear someone's cross, or shoulder their own:
They share our complaining, our comforts, our cares:
What patience in caring, what courage, is theirs!

Rejoice in God's saints, today and all days!
A world without saints forgets how to praise.
In loving, in living, they prove it is true:
Their way of self-giving, Lord, leads us to you.

Originally, to a commission from the Dean of Norwich, Fred wrote two processional hymns for the six-hundredth anniversary celebrations of Mother Julian's *Revelations of Divine Love*. These had necessarily to deal with the cloistered life. Fred then wrote a four-verse hymn based on these two, but still retaining the circumscribed view of sainthood.

In October 1977, he rewrote this to widen its scope, on the advice of John Wilson, who was at the time an adviser to the group responsible for *Broadcast Praise*, the supplement to the *BBC Hymn-Book*. It was sung for the first time on BBC Radio 4 in *The Daily Service* on Monday 21st September 1981. This hymn, also published in *More Hymns for Today*, can be sung on many occasions besides the specifics of All Saints' and Wesley Days to the tune of the OLD 104TH.

The second of the two Julian hymns is still sung in its original form in Julian circles and is included in the section of *Hymns for Special Occasions* (**125**).

53 Sign of Hope

6.6.6.6.6.8 8.

Lord God, when we complain:
'Your Kingdom tarries long,
The Gods of darkness reign,
And there's no end to wrong'—
Show us how many serve you still
And daily seek to do your will.

How many a saint contrives,
Against all odds, to give
Fresh hope to broken lives
And makes the gospel live!
God bids our doubting minds look up
And welcome every sign of hope.

How many a life is spent
In righting human wrongs!
Divine their discontent
Who turn our sighs to songs
And taking courage in their hands
Show us the way to promised lands.

With all who would be free
We bind ourselves to work
For that one world we see
Emerging from the dark,
Till every human right is won,
And all Christ died to do is done.

The Overseas Division of the Methodist Church in Great Britain requested this hymn for a Christian Celebration of International Women's Year in the Royal Albert Hall, London on 9th October 1975 when it was sung to HAREWOOD. Fred's ninth scrapbook wryly observes that the lights were not turned up sufficiently for the Albert Hall audience to see such small print.

54 God is our Song
10 10.10 10.

**The Lord is my strength and song;
and he is become my salvation. (Psalm 118, 14 RV)**

God is our Song, and every singer blest
Who, praising him, finds energy and rest.
All who praise God with unaffected joy
Give back to us the wisdom we destroy.

God is our Song, for Jesus comes to save;
While praising him we offer all we have.
New songs we sing, in ventures new unite,
When Jesus leads us upward into light.

This is the Song no conflict ever drowns;
Who praises God the wrath of man disowns.
Love knows what rich complexities of sound
God builds upon a simple, common ground.

God is our Silence when no songs are sung,
When ecstasy or sorrow stills the tongue.
Glorious the faith which silently obeys
Until we find again the voice of praise.

Fred began to work on this text in 1974 in response to John Wilson's request for new words to Gustav Holst's CHILSWELL, but was not satisfied with it. So it was a real surprise when Erik Routley chose if for *Westminster Praise*, a supplement published in 1976 for the use of Westminster Choir College, Princeton, USA.

55 A Song of Salvation

8.6.8.6.D.
(Version excluding * lines).

Salvation! there's no better word
For what Christ does for me:
He saves me from repented sins
And sets my spirit free.
*   But if in this I rest content
*   How can I hope to see
*   The glorious, utmost consequence
*   Of all Christ asks of me?
O save me absolutely, Lord,
That I may play my part
As your disciple, daily more
Mature in mind and heart!

Salvation! there's no better word
For what Christ offers us—
The love that died for you and me
Upon a Roman cross.
* But if we pass life's victims by,
* How can we hope to learn
* The glorious, utmost consequence
* Of Christ's divine concern?
As servants of your Kingdom, Lord,
O never let us rest
Until your love and justice reach
The needy and oppressed!

Salvation! there's no better word
For all Christ came to do:
His peace removes the barricades
And lets forgiveness through.
* But while we shut our brethren out
* How shall we all attain
* The glorious, utmost consequence
* Of Christ's redeeming reign?
O fill your universal Church
With wisdom, Lord, and love;
And save this power-hungry world
With power from above!

An ecumenical group of young Christians calling themselves *Reflection* have played a significant role in the format of worship experiment since the seventies. Whilst their musicians are caught up in the idiom of contemporary religious music, they always ask searching questions about the 'why?' of Christian worship and are never content for a catchy tune to hide an inappropriate or banal text. In 1974, the Home Mission Division of the Methodist Church commissioned a record from *Reflection* called *Sounds of Salvation*. A congregational hymn on the theme *Salvation Today* was the commission to Fred. The Connexional Secretary, Jeffrey Harris, in writing:

We are thinking more widely than salvation in terms of personal sin.

enclosed a quotation from the Bangkok Conference, showing a more comprehensive nature of the understanding of Salvation than would be traditional amongst people called Methodists.

The tune JOB was chosen for the recording which, Fred notes in his eighth scrapbook, is excellent. The hymn was printed in a simplified version omitting lines marked * in *Partners in Praise* to TANA, an arrangement by Kenneth Fox (see **82**) of a tune he heard in Kenya PETERSHAM is another possibility.

56 One God and Father

8.6 8.6 8.

One God and Father of us all!
This gospel we proclaim
Afresh today, in that one Name
We Christians proudly bear,
In that one faith we meet to share:

One God who is above us all!
Yet we believe it true
This mighty God is working through
What we think weak and small,
And never is beyond our call.

One God, who is within us all!
Believing this, we see
The whole world as one family,
And each dividing wall
A challenge to us, till it fall.

One God and Father of us all!
So we must never cease
To strive, within the bond of peace,
In home, and Church and State
To serve this God we celebrate.

This text was originally written for a Women's Rally in the London Borough of Croydon in 1975 with a tune HIGHLEIGH by Ida Prins-Buttle. High Leigh is a Conference Centre where the annual conference of the Methodist Church Music Society in Great Britain has often met. The simplified version above, in an unusual metre, awaits a tune.

The original version had a sixth line in each verse:

Verse 1: One God and Father of us all!
Verse 2: And never is beyond our call.
Verse 3: A challenge to us, till it fall.
Verse 4: One God and Father of us all!

57 A Prayer for Communicators

8.7.8.7.
(Trochaic)

Lord of every art and science,
Source of all creative skill,
Help us use all kinds of media
For the doing of your will.

So may those who mould opinion
Help us get our values right,
And the artist's private vision
Sharpen our defective sight.

All the lines are open to us,
All resources we require:
May the world of our creation
Be the one that you inspire.

This text on an unusual but highly relevant theme was written in 1975 for a service for journalists, artists and broadcasters in Guildford Cathedral, England, in February 1976. Suggested tunes are LAUS DEO, DRAKES BROUGHTON, HALTON HOLGATE. In the original version, it had as its second verse:

'Whatsoever's just and loving,
Whatsoever's true and pure':
Only to our smooth evasions
Is your simple word obscure.

58 A Hymn for use in Later Life

L.M.

Now praise the hidden God of Love,
In whom we all must live and move,
Who shepherds us, at every stage,
Through youth, maturity, and age:

Who challenged us, when we were young
To storm the citadels of wrong;
In care for others taught us how
God's true community must grow:

Who bids us never lose our zest,
Though age is urging us to rest,
But proves to us that we have still
A work to do, a place to fill.

Then talk no more of wasted time,
But Godward look, and upward climb,
Content to sleep, when day is done,
And rise refreshed, and travel on.

This hymn was written in 1975 as an entry for a competition sponsored by the Hymn Society of America for a hymn which could be sung in later life by Christians and non-Christians believing in a living God. Considering the average age of many congregations, it seems important that some hymns should knit especially with the experience of the elderly. Tunes: SOMERSET HILLS (by Lee Hastings Bristol, Jnr.), ALSTONE and BOW BRICKHILL.

59 The Future Life

8 8.7 7.8.8.

Rest in peace, earth's journey ended,
You whom Christ redeemed, defended:
To the place where saints are one
Safely brought by him alone—
May he grant us like protection—
Rest in peace, earth's journey ended.

Happy soul, to Christ united,
Calmer now and clearer-sighted:
Your new journey now begins,
Freed from earth's besetting sins:
Pressing on towards perfection
Happy soul, to Christ united.

May we meet, dear Lord, in heaven,
Each forgiving, each forgiven,
Each more gifted to pursue
All you have for us to do.
By your Spirit's sure direction
May we meet, dear Lord, in heaven.

This was written in response to a request from Martin Ellis for a new text, as yet unpublished, for a setting by Schubert of a *Litany for All Souls' Day*. Fred feels, however, that with the right tune, it might have use as a hymn as well as an anthem.

60 A Lullaby

7.7.7.7.6.7.

Winter's here, with falling snow:
Lullaby, my little man,
There's no sound or echo now
Where the children leapt and ran:
Lullaby, lullaby,
Where the children leapt and ran.

Light a lantern, hang it high:
Lullaby, my little son,
So that travellers passing by
Think of home and hasten on:
Lullaby, lullaby,
Think of home and hasten on.

Dark it is; but that one star
Lullaby, sing lullaby,
Knows where all the children are,
Though they in a manger lie:
Lullaby, lullaby,
Though they in a manger lie.

Baptist organist, the late Walter Webber, two of whose tunes appeared in the Baptist Supplement *Praise for Today*, responded to Fred's invitation to send him a tune for this lullaby. The composer described the melody as 'floating into' his head—inspired by a reading on the radio of Thomas Hardy's *Far from the Madding Crowd*. Fred, who had written the words equally effortlessly, was delighted by the tune: CONGRESBURY CAROL.

This carol formed Fred's 'do-it-yourself' Christmas Card to his friends in 1974 and was printed in the *Methodist Recorder* of 4th December, 1975.

61 A Thanksgiving for Farmers

7.6.7.6.

When loaves are on the table,
Who sees a field of wheat?
Or thinks about the farmer
Who grew the food we eat?

Perhaps in bitter weather
He had to plough and sow,
As gulls behind the tractor
Reminded him of snow.

And while the seeds were hidden
Beneath the frozen earth,
He had to trust to nature
To mother them at birth.

He watched for those diseases
That harm the tender grain,
And feared to see his acres
Lie rotting in the rain.

But there's a joy of harvest
That everyone may know:
The happiness of reaping
The best that we can grow.

When food is on the table.
And there is bread to eat,
Thank God for every farmer
Who has a field of wheat.

The editor of the Anglican Board of Education wrote to several hymn-writers early in 1976 seeking material for their publication *Together for Festivals*. This is one of two hymns Fred submitted. As tunes in the simple metre 7.6.7.6. are scarce, he asked Stanley Fuller to write one (JONGENS).

The hymn was first sung (to KNECHT) at Harvest Festival at St. Mary's Church, Diss, Norfolk on 26th September, 1976 when Fred preached the sermon. Diss is a charming old market town and its church has an imposing array of fifteenth-century windows. Fred remembers the day well—his scrapbook records 'A memorable Sunday!'.

62 The Festival of the First-Fruits   7.6.7.6.
Deuteronomy 26, 1-15

Come, sing a song of harvest,
Of thanks for daily food!
To offer God the first-fruits
Is old as gratitude.

Long, long ago, the reapers,
Before they kept the feast,
Put first-fruits in a basket,
And took it to the priest.

Shall we, sometimes forgetful
Of where creation starts,
With science in our pockets
Lose wonder from our hearts?

May God, the great Creator,
To whom all life belongs,
Accept these gifts we offer,
Our service and our songs.

And lest the world go hungry
While we ourselves are fed,
Make each of us more ready
To share our daily bread.

This hymn was the second carol written in 1976 for *Together for Festivals*. It fits the English traditional melody of the CHERRY TREE CAROL. It, too, was first used at Harvest Thanksgiving at Diss Parish Church.

63 A Carol for the Sunday After Christmas

There's snow on the mountain and ice on the pond;
The Wise Men are home now in the back of beyond;
The Shepherds have left us; the heavens are dumb;
There's no one to tell us why Jesus has come.

The tree drops its needles, a sign we must go;
But the long road to Egypt is covered in snow;
And wherever we travel the food will be dear:
Who knows what's before us this coming New Year?

But God's in his heaven, and Jesus has come
To show every sinner he's welcome back home,
To be this world's Saviour from hunger and fear,
And give us new courage to face the New Year.

Fred wrote some years later:

> I note that I have used the Nativity Story and its symbols and
> associations rather oddly—but this is how it 'came to me' with
> an unusual degree of spontaneity. But it may puzzle others as it
> now surprises me!

It was with equivalent spontaneity that the editors of *The Galliard Book
of Carols* felt this text caught perfectly the mood of everyday Christians on the
Sunday after Christmas. The text was originally inspired by the charming
tune NEW COURAGE, written by the late Stanley Mountford as an
alternative setting of *Away in a Manger*. Stanley Mountford was for many
years the organist at Birmingham Methodist Central Hall, England. Fred's
carol, with the Mountford tune, was printed in the *Methodist Recorder* and
used as Fred's 'do-it-yourself' Christmas Card for 1976. Allen Percival,
Executive Chairman of the publishing house of Stainer & Bell Ltd and
formerly Principal of the Guildhall School of Music and Drama, wrote the
tune AFTER CHRISTMAS for *The Galliard Book of Carols*.

64 How Blest is He Who Comes

6.6.8.6.7.6.

Let us rejoice in Christ,
Whose Kingdom is at hand!
He comes to be the Lord of Life
In every life and land.
Hosanna in the highest!
How blest is he who comes!

When, lowly-born, he came,
For us condemned to die,
They brought him to Jerusalem
With this triumphant cry:
Hosanna in the highest!
How blest is he who comes!

Rejoice that now he comes
In those who walk his way,
To make this stricken world his own,
And every day his day.
Hosanna in the highest!
How blest is he who comes!

Then let us yield to him
The loyalty he claims,
And never cease to celebrate
The Name above all names.
Hosanna in the highest:
The Name above all names!

This began life as an attempt to set words to Richard Dirksen's VINEYARD HAVEN for use at the Hymn Society's Act of Praise in 1977. But, despite four attempts, Fred could not produce the text John Wilson was seeking. (A rare failure!) Part of the original, however, proved suitable for a Methodist Music Festival later that year in Bath Abbey for which Ida Prins-Buttle wrote an elaborate setting SEFULA.

65 Carol of Five Questions

5.4 4 4.8.

Where shall we lay him,
Helpless and small?
Here is this stall,
This humble stall:
He who is lowly shall not fall.

How shall we feed him,
So he shall rest?
Milk from the breast,
His mother's breast:
Nurtured by love is always best.

What shall we call him
Born this dark night?
Call him the Light,
Call him the Light!
He comes to give us back our sight.

Who then shall heed him,
In time to be?
His two or three,
His two or three:
All who obey his 'Follow me!'

What shall befall him,
Lying so still?
For good or ill,
For good or ill?
Only what lies in the Father's will.

This carol was written in response to a request from the Editor of the *Methodist Recorder* for a carol for the Christmas issue of 1977. It was then submitted with the tune ICENI, especially written for the text by Methodist minister Cyril Hambly, then based at Swaffham, Norfolk. For this tune, the last line of each verse is repeated.

66   Discipleship

8 8.6.D.

Luke 5, 1–11

Lord, when you singled out the Three,
That day of days, by Galilee,
They did not ask or know
Exactly what 'to follow' meant,
To what new aims they gave assent,
Or where they had to go.

In simple faith they followed you,
Because, instinctively, they knew
Whom they could love and trust;
And risked the future for your sake,
And trod the road you had to take,
As all disciples must.

So, when we meet you on that shore,
And hear your voice demanding more
Than we have thought to give:
Then may we know, as they once knew
Beyond all doubt, that following you
Is how we want to live.

Philip Hill, Director of Music of Seaford College, sent Fred the tune
LAVINGTON to which he set this text in 1978. It was accepted for *Partners
in Praise*.

67 Roman Soldiers Marching

7.6.7.6.D.
(Trochaic)

Dark against an eastern sky,
Roman soldiers marching;
No one cheered as they went by,
Roman soldiers marching.
Disciplined to beat their foe,
Roman soldiers marching:
As a boy he watched them go,
Jesus watched them marching.

Jewish boy beside the Way
Watched the soldiers marching;
They will come another day,
Roman soldiers marching.
Then with orders to fulfil,
Roman soldiers marching,
They will hang him on a hill,
Roman soldiers watching.

He who dies is Lord of all,
He shall reign for ever;
Empires rise and empires fall,
He shall reign for ever.
When he comes, our Prince of Peace,
He shall reign for ever;
All oppression then shall cease,
He shall reign for ever!

The original four-verse version was written in 1975 to a tune RAYENS CROSS, sent by Walter Webber. Its second verse then read:

> Every man prepares to die
> Roman soldiers marching
> Down with Parthia! is their cry
> Roman soldiers marching
> Every battle is the last
> Roman soldiers marching
> Pax Romana cannot last
> Roman soldiers marching.

A fellow hymn-writer and Minister of the United Reformed Church in Stamford, Basil Bridge, asked by Fred to comment on his draft, suggested a review of the order of ideas within the hymn—which led to the present version. He also contributed what Fred described as a brilliant suggestion: the amendment of 'marching' to 'watching' in the last line of the new verse 2. 'Biblical, of course, too', noted Basil Bridge.

The text was printed in the *Methodist Recorder* of 1st September 1977 where the suggested tune was TEMPUS ADEST FLORIDUM, the 'Good King Wenceslas' melody. Fred recorded a first known use in public worship in a Glasgow Methodist Church on 30th October 1977. The following May, it found an appropriate use in Scotland as the opening hymn at the Annual Display of the 5th Cumbernauld Boys' Brigade Junior 'A' Section in Abronhill Parish Church. The hymn is published in *Partners in Praise* to SOLDIERS MARCHING, a tune written sometime earlier for the text by David McCarthy. It is printed with an accompaniment for optional instruments as well as piano or guitar.

68 Easter Day

7.7.7.7.D.
(Trochaic)

> Look! the sun awakes the sky,
> Rolls the stone of night away!
> Wake the world with carols! Cry:
> Jesus lives! It's Easter Day!
> You who sorrow, you who doubt,
> You who sin and you who stray,
> You who ask what life's about:
> Jesus lives! It's Easter Day!

83

Happy they who ran to test
News too good to be believed!
Happy they who have confessed
It was unbelief deceived;
Happy they who, sad at heart,
Turned their feet Emmaus way!
Where hope ends is where we start;
Jesus lives! It's Easter Day!

Neighbours, let us not give way
To defeat or to despair;
Never now need sin have sway
Over lives beyond repair.
Never now shall death deny
Life it is has final say!
Wake the world with carols! Cry:
Jesus lives! It's Easter Day!

This challenge came in 1975 from Alan Luff, then Vicar of Penmaenmawr, writing as Secretary of the Hymn Society of Great Britain and Ireland. He is now Precentor of Westminster Abbey.

> In getting heated up about Easter I always bear in mind Vaughan Williams' comment in his essay on Beethoven's 9th: 'It is admittedly harder to write good music which is joyful than that which is sad'. That last sentence is marvellous and probably applies to words, too.

Another Alan, Fred's Methodist colleague in the ordained ministry, Alan Dale, famed for *New World* and *Winding Quest* wrote about a conference that Easter (1975) reporting a possible first singing of the hymn:

> Look! the sun awakes the sky and Catholic and Protestant voices sang lustily in unison. We were all one in its joy.

The tune which inspired Fred was RESURREXIT by Stanley Fuller. It also goes well to RILEY and has been published as an anthem by the American composer, Jack Schrader, issued by Hope Publishing Company.

69 At a Retreat

7.7.7.6.

Daily we come, dear Master,
To springs of living water,
And daily you sustain us
With your refreshing word.

Keep us alert to danger,
And by your love protect us
From sins that lie in waiting
To snatch us from your side.

Deeper than our rejoicing,
Our praises and our praying,
In an unbroken silence
Your inner voice is heard.

Alone, or brought together,
In praying you prepare us
To give you daily service
In your demanding world.

This hymn for occasions when we withdraw from the business of life still
needs a tune for its unusual rhythm.

70 The Gracious Invitation

8.7.8.7.8.7.
(Trochaic)

His the gracious invitation:
'Come and be my honoured guest;
Share my joyful celebration:
Love alone shall be the test:
Lose no time in hesitation,
Come and be forever blest!'

There the faithful see their Master
In a pure, unclouded light;
Saints, apostles, prophets, martyrs,
In his praises all unite;
Nothing there shall ever part us
From a Love that's infinite.

Martin Ellis, Assistant Director of Music at Taunton School, asked Fred in 1977 for an English text for Fauré's anthem, *Tantum Ergo*. This is also suitable as a Communion hymn. A suggested tune is GRAFTON.

71 Confirmation and Commitment

11.10.11.10.
(Dactylic)

Lord, we have come at your own invitation,
Chosen by you, to be counted your friends;
Yours is the strength that sustains dedication,
Ours a commitment we know never ends.

Here, at your table, confirm our intention,
Give it your seal of forgiveness and grace;
Teach us to serve, without pride or pretension,
Lord, in your Kingdom, whatever our place.

When, at your table, each time of returning,
Vows are renewed and our courage restored:
May we increasingly glory in learning
All that it means to accept you as Lord.

So, in the world, where each duty assigned us
Gives us the chance to create or destroy,
Help us to make those decisions that bind us,
Lord, to yourself, in obedience and joy.

This text came out of a request by Martin Ellis, in 1977, for a hymn to be sung at Taunton School Confirmation Service. In its original version, it was written in two verses of eight lines for S. S. Wesley's tune EPIPHANY. The third line of the hymn ended 'our vocation'. The four-verse form was prepared for the family worship book *Partners in Praise* for which Methodist minister, Brian Coleman, wrote the new tune CONFIRMATION.

An American version has a second verse amended chiefly to meet the reasonable objection that in the Episcopal Church 'seal' is used of Baptism, not of the grace received in Holy Communion:

> Here, at your table, confirm our intention
> Ever to cherish the gifts you provide;
> Teach us to serve without pride or pretension,
> Led by your Spirit, defender and guide.

72 A Hymn for the Nation

15 15 15.7.

It is God who holds the nations in the hollow of his hand;
It is God whose light is shining in the darkness of the land;
It is God who builds his City on the Rock and not on sand:
May the living God be praised!

It is God whose purpose summons us to use the present hour;
Who recalls us to our senses when a nation's life turns sour;
In the discipline of freedom we shall know his saving power:
May the living God be praised!

When a thankful nation, looking back, has cause to celebrate
Those who win our admiration by their service to the state;
When self-giving is a measure of the greatness of the great:
May the living God be praised!

He reminds us every sunrise that the world is ours on lease—
For the sake of life tomorrow, may our love for it increase;
May all races live together, share its riches, be at peace:
May the living God be praised!

Fred's *A Hymn for the Nation*, written in 1976, began life as a local commission for use in Norwich Cathedral during the celebrations of the Queen's Silver Jubilee the following year. It came as a complete surprise when he heard from the Archbishop of Canterbury's senior chaplain that serious consideration was being given to including the hymn in the official Order of Service agreed by representatives of all the Churches. So it came to be sung throughout Britain and in many parts of the Commonwealth. The fact that it was said in the Press to have ousted Sir John Betjeman's poem for the occasion, and much was made of this on radio and television, caused Fred real distress at the time.

When a letter from Harry Eskew, editor of *The Hymn*, pointed out that *A Hymn for the Nation* was just as suitable for the Americas, Fred slightly revised the third verse to give it wider reference. The opening lines of verse 3 read originally:

> When a thankful nation, looking back, unites to celebrate
> Those who reign in our affection by their service to the state.

Fred's fourteenth scrapbook contains this light literary comment from J. E. Bowers, his hymn-writer friend, the Rural Dean of Ashby-de-la-Zouch, headed 'First and final draft':

A HYMN IN PRAISE OF HYMNOGRAPHERS

It was on a Monday lunch-time,
Cold the day, but bright the sun;
On the table our transistor
Turned to 'The World at One'.

Slumping pound and striking workers ...
How the news seems quite obscene!
Suddenly I heard th' announcer
Saying 'Rev'rend Fred Pratt Green'!

Fred Pratt Green? My ears deceive me;
Our Fred on the BBC?
Ah, of course! the hymn he's written
For our dear Queen's Jubilee.

Betjeman's hymn is more a poem
(This is what the critics say);
Our Fred's hymn is just the ticket
For this special Royal Day.

Thank you, Fred, for splendid verses,
(Written for the Norwich Dean)
Which (praise Lambeth!) we'll be singing
To the praise of Britain's Queen.

The tune to which the hymn was sung, on radio and television, and in the churches, was VISION by Walford Davies, a former Master of the King's Music, in an arrangement by John Wilson. An anthem setting by Austin Lovelace is issued by Hope Publishing Company.

73 Good News

6.6 6.4.8 8.4.

God saw that it was good;
Yet, being God, knew all
That would in time befall
This world of ours:
When he created out of dust,
By evolution's patient thrust,
Its first pale flowers.

Now, shocked by what we are,
We cry, in our dismay,
Had God no better way
To foster life:
Than give us freedom to destroy
What he intended for our joy
In senseless strife?

So let us hear good news!
He comes to seek the lost,
For, being Love, he must
Himself give all,
And of divine necessity,
Reach out his hands to us, and die
To break our fall.

89

Dear God, in whom we trust,
Deliver us at last
From our repented past,
Our present plight;
And strengthen us to recreate
Through Christ, in spite of greed and hate,
Your world of light.

This hymn was written for the Methodist Church Music Society Conference of 1976 when Martin Ellis asked for words to S. S. Wesley's tune WIGAN for a lecture about the composer. The text was published in *The Expository Times*.

74 The Eternal Mystery

14 14.13 13.14 14.

We come to worship you, O Lord, whose glory is so great
We lose you in the magnitude of things which you create;
But when we walk in Springtime, or watch the stars at night,
We find you in earth's beauty, in patterns of delight;
Until the latest news breaks in, of famine or of flood:
And, oh! We wish you were a God whose ways we understood.

So help us worship you in Christ, to us both God and Man,
Whose love has been the light of life since life itself began;
Who taught the truths that free us from the evils we abhor,
Who made his cross an act of faith, and lives for evermore
To give to those who follow him, in days when doubts increase,
A share in God's deep purposes, and keeps us in his peace.

This hymn was especially commissioned in 1977 by Philip Hill for a new hymn and service book for Seaford College near Petworth in Sussex. THAXTED was specified as a tune which the school enjoyed singing and which might gain wider use with a new text.

75 Holy Lord

8.7.8.7.8.7.
(Trochaic)

Loving Lord, as now we gather,
Of that love unworthy still,
Give us courage to surrender
Rebel heart and stubborn will,
And in us, in faith maturing,
All your promises fulfil.

Holy Lord, as here you give us
Bread and wine, as means of grace,
Grant to every true believer
Now to meet you face to face,
And to own, in silent wonder,
Lord, how holy is this place.

© 1982. For permission to reproduce this text, see page ii.

This text was also commissioned in 1977 by Martin Ellis, who wanted English words for Louis Vierne's *Tantum Ergo*. It can be sung, however, as a simple communion hymn to LEWES.

76 The Church of Christ

8.7.8.7.D.
(Trochaic)

God is here! As we his people
Meet to offer praise and prayer,
May we find in fuller measure
What it is in Christ we share.
Here, as in the world around us,
All our varied skills and arts
Wait the coming of his Spirit
Into open minds and hearts.

Here are symbols to remind us
Of our lifelong need of grace;
Here are table, font and pulpit;
Here the cross has central place.
Here in honesty of preaching,
Here in silence, as in speech,
Here, in newness and renewal,
God the Spirit comes to each.

Here our children find a welcome
In the Shepherd's flock and fold,
Here as bread and wine are taken,
Christ sustains us as of old,
Here the servants of the Servant
Seek in worship to explore
What it means in daily living
To believe and to adore.

Lord of all, of Church and Kingdom,
In an age of change and doubt,
Keep us faithful to the gospel,
Help us work your purpose out.
Here, in this day's dedication,
All we have to give, receive:
We, who cannot live without you,
We adore you! we believe!

In 1978, Russell Schulz-Widmar, Co-director of Music at University United
Methodist Church, Austin, Texas wrote:

We are in need of a hymn. It would be sung for the first time at the closing service of an eight-month long festival centering round the themes of Worship, Music and the Arts.... The closing Service of this festival will center around the dedication of new reading desks, communion table, and font, and finally, the rededication of the people to the life commanded of us and given through Jesus Christ.... We would prefer a metre of 8.7.8.7.D. since we could then use your text to introduce the tune ABBOT'S LEIGH to our congregation.

The hymn Fred wrote has already proved to be useful elsewhere. Almost immediately it was sung at the Service of Dedication of a new building for the First Presbyterian Church also in Austin, Texas. Subsequently the hymn has appeared in *Partners in Praise*, *More Hymns for Today* and *Songs of Thanks and Praise*. A setting of Cyril Taylor's ABBOT'S LEIGH with these words for choir and brass, arranged by Austin Lovelace is to be published by OUP. As well as ABBOT'S LEIGH, the hymn may be sung to BLAENWERN.

77 Jesus Lord of Glory   8 6.8 6.8 6.5 5.5 5.5 5.6.

Jesus is the Lord of Glory:
Reign in me Lord Jesus!
Jesus is the Light of the World:
Shine in me, Lord Jesus!
Jesus is the Friend of sinners:
Set me free, Lord Jesus!
Jesus is the Way:
May I walk in it!
Jesus is the Truth:
May I believe in it!
Jesus is the Life:
May I share in it!
Way and Truth and Life.

© 1979. For permission to reproduce this text, see page ii.

This arrangement of scriptural texts was made by Fred to meet a particular need for *Partners in Praise*. Fellow Methodist Minister Brian Coleman provided a lively tune KERUGMA.

78 A Hymn for Mothering Sunday

S.M.

How great the debt we owe
To those who love us most;
They give us birth, and help us grow,
And rarely count the cost.

To make us feel secure
They lose their life in ours;
And what they mean to us is more
Than we can say with flowers.

How can we measure love?
Yet treasure it we must
For what God gives us from above
Is held by us in trust.

Then let us vow today,
As those who know love's worth,
To love, to worship, and obey
The Lord of all the earth.

This hymn was written in March 1978 to meet a gap in the Family Worship Book, *Partners in Praise*. It was broadcast during an Act of Worship at Heswell Methodist Church in the Wirral on Mothering Sunday 1980, to the tune FRANCONIA. See **156** for *A Carol for Mothering Sunday*.

79 Song of the Christians

8.5.7.6.9.7.9.6.

There are songs for us all to sing—
Sing them loud and clear:
Songs of joy and hope and peace,
Of courage and good cheer.
As the love of the Lord floods our hearts
This is where our worship starts:
With the song of praise creation sings
To all with ears to hear.

There's a song for us all to sing—
Sing it loud and clear:
It's the gospel song we sing
All seasons of the year.
How the Word became flesh for our sakes;
Of the difference Easter makes;
It's the song of joy we Christians sing
To all with ears to hear.

There's a song for us all to sing—
Sing it loud and clear:
It's the song we sinners sing
As the Lord of life draws near;
When the sheep that is lost will be found;
And the son is homeward bound;
It's the song of hope we Christians sing
To all with ears to hear.

There's a song for us all to sing—
Sing it loud and clear:
It's the song we are bold to sing
Of the love that casts out fear;
Of the Spirit who makes us all one;
And of freedom to be won;
It's the song of peace we Christians sing
To all with ears to hear.

Brian Coleman, much of whose ministry has been spent in the role of School Chaplain but who was then minister of Punshon Memorial Church, Bournemouth, wrote a delightful tune SONG OF PRAISE for possible use to another text in *Partners in Praise*. Fred wrote this text in 1978 following a vain search to find an item with which to open this hymn-book for all ages worshipping together. The hymn opened the *Sunday Half-Hour* broadcast from Chalkwell Park Methodist Church, Westcliff-on-Sea, Essex in December 1980.

80 Where Two or Three...

6.5.6.4.

An Introit

As we Christians gather,
Joyfully we give
Glory to the Father:
Alleluia!

Few or more in number,
Christ is in the midst,
Whom we now remember:
Alleluia!

Now the Holy Spirit
Offers what is his—
Life, if we desire it:
Alleluia!

Valerie Ruddle wrote THORPE originally for Fred's *After darkness, light* but it seemed ill-suited, and Fred responded to the suggestion that words suitable for an Introit might fit the mood of the tune better. This was published in the *Methodist Recorder* in 1978.

81 The Threefold Truth

6.6.6.6.3.4.5.

This is the threefold truth
On which our faith depends;
And with this joyful cry
Worship begins and ends:
Christ has died!
Christ is risen!
Christ will come again!

Made sacred by long use,
New-minted for our time,
Our liturgies sum up
The hope we have in him:
Christ has died!
Christ is risen!
Christ will come again!

On this we fix our minds
As, kneeling side by side,
We take the bread and wine
From him, the Crucified:
Christ has died!
Christ is risen!
Christ will come again!

By this we are upheld
When doubt and grief assails
Our Christian fortitude,
And only grace avails:
Christ has died!
Christ is risen!
Christ will come again!

This is the threefold truth
Which, if we hold it fast,
Changes the world and us
And brings us home at last.
Christ has died!
Christ is risen!
Christ will come again!

The threefold acclamation which ends each verse finds a place in many recent liturgies but comes from ancient sources. The impression which this triad made upon Fred led him to write this text. It is set, in anthem form, by the American composer Jack Schrader (issued by Hope Publishing Company) but Fred hopes someone will write a tune for it in the form of a hymn.

97

82 For Those in Captivity
Psalm 137

8.6.8.6.D.
(D.C.M.)

'How can we sing our songs of faith
In this far, foreign land?'
The exiles cried, and knew that God,
Their God, would understand.
'We'll hang our harps on willow trees
Until the day shall come
When God shall set the captives free,
And send his People home.'

Yet sing they did; as captives must
When faith in God is strong;
And Christians in an alien world
Take courage from their song.
So negro slaves, in Egypt's land,
Sang 'Let my people go!'
And saints in concentration camps
Sang hymns, as we do now.

Let us, who have our freedom still,
And know what it is worth,
Remember those unjustly held
In any cell on earth.
May God deliver them, and us,
From every tyranny
That shamefully enslaves our race—
Lord, set your servants free!

Kenneth Fox and his wife were in charge of administration at the Methodist hospital at Maua in Kenya from 1970 to 1972. Their son Peter was Medical Superintendent of the Ngao Methodist Hospital on the Tana River from 1964 to 1971. While in Kenya, Kenneth recorded tunes which he heard locally (including TANA) and asked Fred to write a hymn to use at Missionary talks when he returned home. Now organist and choirmaster of Wesley Church, High Wycombe, he writes:

Psalm 137 and the theme *How shall we sing the Lord's song in a strange land?* is a good text for all who engage in overseas work.

The hymn originally ended:

> May God, our God, deliver us
> From life-destroying sin,
> And set his captive people free,
> And bring his Kingdom in.

The new ending to preserve unity of theme, with its strong final line, was written in 1981.

83 The Suffering Community 10.10.10.10.10 10.

Pray for the Church, afflicted and oppressed,
For all who suffer for the gospel's sake,
That Christ may show us how to serve them best
In that one Kingdom Satan cannot shake.
But how much more than us they have to give,
Who by their dying show us how to live.

Pray for Christ's dissidents, who daily wait,
As Jesus waited in the olive grove,
The unjust trial, the pre-determined fate,
The world's contempt for reconciling love.
Shall all they won for us, at such a cost,
Be by our negligence or weakness lost?

Pray that if times of testing should lay bare
What sort we are, who call ourselves his own,
We may be counted worthy then to wear,
With quiet fortitude, Christ's only crown:
The crown that in his saints he wears again—
The crown of thorns that signifies his reign.

This hymn was written in response to a general appeal for a text on this subject to fit the Lectionary for a possible new Anglican hymn-book. The tune is Orlando Gibbons' SONG I (see also **98**).

84 Christians and Pagans

Men go to God when they are in despair;
They pray to him for help, for peace, for bread,
For mercy when they sin, are sick, or dead.
Christians and pagans, all of us, do this.

Men go to God when they are in despair,
Finding him poor, scorned, homeless, without bread,
Laid low by weight of evil, weak or dead.
We Christians stand by God in his distress.

God goes to man when he is in despair,
Body and spirit feeds he with his bread,
For pagans, as for Christians, he hangs dead.
And all are taught forgiveness by his death.

This was written in 1978 for *Partners in Praise* but the time-scale necessary for clearing copyrights did not allow its inclusion. It is Fred's version of a Bonhoeffer text translated by Geoffrey Winthrop Young. Tunes suggested are STONER HILL or SURSUM CORDA.

85 Peter Speaks

C.M.

One morning on that misty shore
We found a meal prepared,
And ate together one meal more
With him, our risen Lord.

Three times he asked me, face to face,
If I were still his man.
It's thanks to his amazing grace,
Yes, I am still his man!

And if you, too, deny your Lord,
Although it be but once,
You'll hear the same forgiving word
And have your second chance.

For some are called a second time
And some more times than this;
And only those who follow him
Know what all others miss.

When Fred and his co-editor Bernard Braley were seeking to fill gaps for
Partners in Praise, one brief was for something on the Resurrection Story of
the breakfast on a Galilee beach. Bernard also wanted a contemporary text to
the tune AMAZING GRACE. This was an attempt to meet both needs. It
was first sung round the breakfast table at a Communion Service in East
Finchley Methodist Church, London on Whit Sunday 1978. The text can
also be sung to ST. AUSTIN, and has been set to music by Lee Hastings
Bristol, Jnr.

86 The Resurrection and the Life   L.M.

Come, share with us the joyful news:
Our Jesus lives, in death's despite!
For lack of faith, do not refuse
To step from darkness into light.

How dark it was we mourners knew,
Who grieved for him in self-despair;
Until at last the sun broke through,
And it was Jesus standing there!

101

Lay grief aside and dry your eyes;
With life-denying sin have done;
Come, with your Risen Lord, arise:
A new life waits to be begun.

This simple Easter Hymn was written in 1979: the suggested tune is
SOLEMNIS HAEC FESTIVITAS, an Angers Church Melody.

87 The Fall

8.7.8.7.
(Iambic)

A tree there grew in Eden's glade
That bore its fruit in season.
'You must not eat of it!' God said,
And gave the strongest reason.

How hard we find it to obey!
How close we are to sinning!
Our appetites lead us astray,
And did from life's beginning.

So Man and Woman, weak of will,
Both yielded to temptation:
This paradox confounds us still—
Their fall was our salvation.

If tempted, Lord, may we refuse
All godless ways of living;
Defeated, never may we lose
The fruits of your forgiving.

This hymn, a re-writing of some discarded verse, was prompted in 1979 by the
editor of a possible new Anglican hymn-book who supplied a list of 'gaps' he
hoped to fill. It is intended for the tune ACH GOTT UND HERR.

88 The Remnant

7.6.7.6.D.

The God who sent the prophets
Inspired them for our good,
To help us face the menace
Of evils they withstood.
How faithfully they warn us,
From Israel's stormy past,
That those who sow injustice
Will reap the holocaust.

They say the Judge of nations
Is making all things new;
That when the many fail him,
He saves us by the few.
In this prophetic promise
Our anxious spirits rest;
In them, his chosen Remnant,
The future shall be blessed.

Yet not by being righteous
May we secure our place,
Or think to serve the future
Save in the strength of grace.
For there is but one Saviour.
The One we crucified,
The lonely Suffering Servant
Who calls us to his side.

As with **87**, this hymn was written in October 1979 to fill another gap in the
proposed new Anglican hymn-book. The suggested tune is CRÜGER.

89 Justification by Faith

Lord, I repent my sin
And bow my head in shame,
I am confounded by a God
Who loves me as I am.

I need to justify
My lawlessness and pride;
But now a self within myself
Confesses that I lied.

The sentence I deserve
I now no longer dread:
I know my Judge has died for me,
And bids me raise my head.

He calls me to his side
And counts me with the just:
For when I put my trust in him
He takes me too on trust.

Now justified by faith,
I want my life to prove
There is no greater power on earth
Than God's redeeming love.

When Fred heard again, in 1981, from the editors of the proposed Anglican hymn-book that they were seeking a hymn in present-day language and imagery on the concept of Justification by Faith, he attempted this difficult task. The suggested tune is ST. AUGUSTINE.

90 Partners

8.6.8.6.D.
(D.C.M.)

What joy it is to worship here,
And find ourselves at home,
Where God, who uses every gift,
Has room for all who come!
Yet are no two of us alike
Of all the human race,
And we must seek a common ground
If we would share his grace.

In partnership with all who work
To cure our social ills,
We bring to this community
Our own distinctive skills.
Though now we shut the city out,
Its tensions and despairs,
We, like our Master, care for it
And hold it in our prayers.

So God, each generation, gives
New meaning to his love:
His changing image changes us
And keeps us on the move
Towards the only kingdom where
All truths, all cultures, meet
And our unlikeness is his way
Of making heaven complete.

This text was written at the request of the members of East Finchley
Methodist Church in London on the occasion of the re-opening of their
church as a flexible working space, and with a request that the hymn should
emphasise the integration of persons of diverse cultures and outlooks. It was
duly sung in September 1980. The suggested tune is TYROL.

91 Our Daily Work

6.6.6.6.8 8.

Lord God, in whom all worlds,
All life, all work, began;
Give us faith to know
We serve your master plan.
How happy they who thus have found
Contentment in the daily round.

But when good work receives
No adequate reward;
When meaningless routines
Leave willing workers bored;
When time is spent in needless strife;
Make us ashamed, O Lord of life.

And if, in leaner years,
What we had gained is lost;
If progress must be bought
At someone else's cost:
Make us, one nation, swift to share
The hardships others have to bear.

So, for tomorrow's sake
Teach us new skills today,
To do your perfect will
In our imperfect way,
And live as those whom you have called
To be your work-force in the world.

This hymn, written in December 1979, won first prize in a competition sponsored by the Industrial Christian Fellowship for a hymn or song on the theme of our daily work. Valerie Ruddle wrote a tune TRAVAIL. Later Fred changed the last two lines of verse 1, which originally read:

How happy they who thus can find
Contentment in the daily grind.

Explaining the change, Fred wrote to Hereward Cooke, Director of the Fellowship:

> I had no idea, when I started to write hymns, what pitfalls await the hymn-writer!

> My friend Alan Webster, Dean of St. Paul's, tells me he was unable to use *Our Daily Work* because he was assured that 'daily grind' has sexual overtones in Lancashire! As a son of that happy-go-lucky county this was news to me!

It did seem, however, it might be wise to revise the hymn to meet this complaint, even though 'daily grind' has become 'daily round' with obvious loss of impact.

In replying, Hereward Cooke wrote:

> I had originally thought that the phrase 'daily grind' was most suitable in connection with daily work where so many ambiguities and imperfections naturally exist. I don't actually think that the Almighty would have been offended if the phrase in some people's minds meant something other than what you intended.

Tunes suggested include CROFT'S 148TH and CHRISTCHURCH. Michael Dawney also set the text to OUR DAILY WORK in 1981.

92 Our Christian Vocation

8.6.88.66.

How clear is our vocation, Lord,
When once we heed your call:
To live according to your word,
And daily learn, refreshed, restored,
That you are Lord of all.
And will not let us fall.

107

But if, forgetful, we should find
Your yoke is hard to bear;
If worldly pressures fray the mind,
And love itself cannot unwind
Its tangled skein of care:
Our inward life repair.

We marvel how your saints become
In hindrances more sure;
Whose joyful virtues put to shame
The casual way we wear your name,
And by our faults obscure
Your power to cleanse and cure.

In what you give us, Lord, to do,
Together or alone,
In old routines and ventures new,
May we not cease to look to you,
The cross you hung upon—
All you endeavoured done

This hymn was inspired by a request in 1980 from Erik Routley for a new text to REPTON and a letter from the Joint Director of Music at University United Methodist Church, Austin, Texas, for a hymn on vocation. Erik contends that REPTON is not a good match with John Whittier's words *Dear Lord and Father of mankind* where it calls for the repetition of the last line of each verse. REPTON of course was not written for the Whittier text but comes from Parry's *Judith*.

In responding to Fred's first draft, Russell Schulz-Widmar criticised two words:

> ... the words are 'own' in the sense 'acknowledge', and 'mark' in the sense of 'take note of'. Both these of course have long histories in hymnic diction but I do see them being removed from American hymnals by editors who believe they are becoming obscure.

Fred altered 'own' to 'learn' in Verse 1, line 4 and 'Mark your saints, how they become' to 'We marvel how your saints become' in Verse 3, line 1.

93 Music-Makers

7.5.7.5.8.7.

Let us praise Creation's Lord
With a thankful heart,
Each interpreting the Word
In our chosen art:
We shall see the glory of God
As the whole fulfils the part.

Music-makers we explore
All the world of sound,
Bringing to another's score
Our attentive mind:
We shall see the glory of God
Where the purest joys are found.

All the universe displays,
God at work and play:
Joy it is to join in praise,
And in silence pray:
And yet see the glory of God
In a still more perfect way.

Life's an art in which we prove
God is worshipped best
When in our creative love
Other lives are blest:
O to see the glory of God
In the face of Jesus Christ!

The hymn was written in 1979 in anticipation of a commission which did not in the end come Fred's way. The tune BEACHENWELL by Cyril Hambly was especially written for the text.

94 The Fall of the Year

11 11.10 10.

Summer is over; the dark fields lie fallow:
See how the poplar turns orange and yellow!
All other seasons have carols to spare:
What shall we sing in the fall of the year?

Morning and evening there's mist in the valley;
Wine-red the berries on hawthorn and holly.
Hark to the robin, how plaintive his air!
What shall we sing in the fall of the year?

Newcomers forage in pasture and furrow;
Squirrels are hoarding their food for tomorrow;
Harvests are gathered: the autumn is here,
Season of fruitfulness, fall of the year.

Sing of fulfilment, contentment, reflection;
Sing, beyond winter, of earth's resurrection.
Sing we this carol, now autumn is here:
Thanks be to God for the fall of the year.

This setting made in 1978 to an old French Carol tune NOUVEL! NOUVEL! GRANDE REJOUISSANCE! reminds us that carols are meant to be sung through the year. One verse of the first draft read:

Swallow and martin have left us for Tunis.
Hark to the robin, how plaintive his tune is!
Winter has Christmas, with carols to share:
What shall we sing in the fall of the year.

The Joint Editors of the *Galliard Book of Carols* responded:

No, you can't have 'Tunis' and 'tune is'... not even you! Besides we're selling the book all over the world and Allen Percival comments that American/Australian swallows seek other summer haunts. But then Australia doesn't have a winter Christmas!!

Another editorial query was whether the robin's song is plaintive, but Fred defended this out of an authoritative book on birds!

Marjorie Green, née Dowsett: Childhood Playtime

Fred Pratt Green: An Edwardian Childhood

Reverend and Mrs. Fred Pratt Green, 1982

The Methodist Conference of 1966 agreed to publication of a Supplement of about 100 Hymns to the present Hymn Book (1933). The G.P. Committee appointed the "Working Party" to make the Selection. Several of us were added after work had begun. W.P. included:-

Rev. Dr. Francis B. Westbrook
Mr. John Wilson (Editor of HCS)
Rev. Gordon S. Wakefield (Editor, Epworth Press)
Rev. Ivor Jones (Secretary)

The Working Party presented its proposed Supplement to G.P. Committee in April 1968. The Conference of 1968 approved.

It was involvement in all the work of the Supplement which got me busy trying to write hymns. Often we found we liked a tune but not the words set to it in other Hymn Books. Because I have written quite a lot of poetry in the last 20 years, I was challenged to meet the need for new words to certain tunes!

"
CHRIST IS THE WORLD'S LIGHT,
HE AND NONE OTHER
"

The Uniqueness of Christ

Christ is the world's Light, he and none other;
Born in our darkness, he became our Brother.
If we have seen him, we have seen the Father:
Glory to God on high.

2 Christ is the world's Peace, he and none other;
No man can serve him and despise his brother.
Who else can make us one in God the Father?
Glory to God on high.

Unites

3 Christ is the world's Life, he and none other;
~~Sold him for silver, murder him, our brother~~
He, who redeems us, reigns with God the Father:
Glory to God on high.

4 Give God the glory, God and none other;
Give God the glory, Spirit, Son and Father;
Give God the glory, God in man my brother:
Glory to God on high.

F. Pratt Green (1903-   )

Tune: CHRISTE SANCTORUM
17th cent. arr. Vaughan Williams (HCS 325)

Sold once for silver, murdered here, our Brother —

See unauthorised reprint of original version

THE TUNE CHRISTE SANCTORUM is set in most Hymn Books either to "Now God be with us for the night is falling" or "Father most holy, merciful and loving". IT CALLS FOR THE SAPPHIC VERSE FORM, which, however excellent in Latin, is not well-suited to the English language owing to its weak (feminine) line endings. In order to avoid this technical problem, I wrote words which fit the tune but are not strictly in the sapphic metre (11.11.11.5), and which strengthen the weak endings of lines 1, 2, 3, by repeating the end words in each verse, and also by giving an emphatic last line. The metre adopted is, in fact: 10.11.11.6.

✱ I gave way on this!
See emendation

John Wilson, whose criticisms are always founded on a sensitive understanding of worship, does not like the 2nd line of the 3rd verse. He calls it a "smash-hit" line, out of tune with the rest of the hymn. He also dislikes it on the ground that it smacks of masochism! One ought not to sing of one's guilt in this way, when one has no intention of doing anything about it. My answer is that the hymn, though very orthodox theologically, has a thread of HUMANISM running through it — an element of protest — that the line follows on reasonably from line 2 of verse 2, & finds its answer in the phrase "God in man my brother" in the last verse.

Dr. Erik Routley prefers the tune ISTE CONFESSOR.

Scrapbook 1, page 6.

Whithorn Priory, Whithorn, Wigtownshire (see **123**)

95 The Advent Season

88.666.

The Church, in Advent, from of old
Has heeded prophets who foretold
Messiah's reign of peace.
Then all our wars shall cease,
Our greed and hatred cease.

Beneath the heel of Greece and Rome
God's People trusted he would come,
In hope of him made strong,
How long, they cried, how long?
O Lord of Hosts, how long?

But now, at last, in God's good time,
Has Mary come to Bethlehem
Our Infant Lord to bear.
He comes as David's heir;
Of all our Kingdoms heir.

And Simeon sees, before he dies,
The Christ long promised by the wise
In prophesies and psalms.
He takes him in his arms,
He folds him in his arms.

These Advent days, with loving care
And childlike joy, we too prepare
Our churches, hearts, and homes.
O welcome, when he comes,
Our Saviour, when he comes.

The text was written in December 1980 at the request of John Wilson to
provide additional words for Francis Westbrook's HARPENDEN. The tune
was originally written for *When Jesus walked by Galilee* to which it is printed
in the Baptist supplement *Praise for Today*.

96 Come, Lord Jesus

8.7.8.7.4.7.
(Trochaic)

Lo! God's Son is now ascended,
God of God and Light of Light.
Nothing he began is ended,
Nothing lost or put to flight.
Do not mourn him,
Gone forever from our sight.

Lo! he sends his promised Spirit,
To be with us evermore;
All that we in Christ inherit
He equips us to explore.
He is mighty
To convert, sustain, restore.

Spirit-led, and signs discerning,
We shall watch his Kingdom grow;
Ready for our Lord's returning,
Though we know not when or how.
Come, Lord Jesus,
To a world that needs you now.

This was written in November 1980 at the request of John Wilson who
wanted an alternative text for HELMSLEY, usually sung with Charles
Wesley's *Lo! he comes with clouds descending*. Erik Routley suggested BRYN
CALFARIA, which fits Fred's words better, and noted that in the United
States of America this Welsh tune is, in some circles, sung to Wesley's words.

97 Ring the Bells

Ring the bells of Bethlehem!
Jesus is born to save us all:
Ring the bells of Bethlehem!
Comes to redeem us from the Fall.
Ring the bells of every town,
There is joy when the lost are found.
Ring the bells in every town,
Let the whole world hear the sound!

Toll a bell in Jerusalem!
Jesus dies to save us all,
Toll a bell in Jerusalem!
Dies to redeem us from the Fall.
Chorus

Ring the bells of Jerusalem!
Jesus lives to save us all:
Ring the bells of Jerusalem!
Lives to redeem us from the Fall.
Chorus

Ring the bells of every town!
Let the whole world hear the sound!
Ring the bells of every town!
There is joy when the lost are found!
Chorus

This text was written in 1978 for the traditional eighteenth-century French Carol IL EST NÉ, LE DIVIN ENFANT as part of Fred's contribution to *The Galliard Book of Carols.*

113

98 A Christmas Song after George Wither L.M.

Thus Angels sung, and thus sing we:
'To God on high all glory be;
Let him on Earth his Peace bestow,
And unto men his favour show.'

Thus Shepherds ran, and thus run we.
The Holy Babe, our Lord, we see;
With joy believe that he doth keep
In safety all his stubborn Sheep.

Thus Wise Men knelt, and thus kneel we.
Let us all creation bow the knee
To him who stooped, in meanest Birth,
To make a Heav'n of our poor Earth.

What Angels sung, and Shepherds saw,
And Wise Men gave in humble awe,
Shall be our Theme, until we see
Our Lord himself, and silent be.

In the seventeenth century the poet George Wither versified what he called *The Hymnes and Songs of the Church*, with tunes by the celebrated composer Orlando Gibbons. One of these was *The Song of the Angels* (Luke 2.14) which only provided material for a single verse—printed in italics above—sung to Gibbons' SONG 34 which became known as ANGELS' SONG. (A facsimile is shown in the introductory essay in *Hymns for Church and School* and all of Wither's book with Gibbons' music is newly edited by David Wulstan in volume 21 of *Early English Church Music*.)

It was John Wilson who, wishing to restore the original association of words and tune, suggested to Fred that he should add three verses in similar style, to provide a new Christmas hymn for use with the original form of the tune. This was sung and broadcast at a Hymn Society Act of Praise at Exeter in July 1980.

99 God's own Son

8 8.8 8.10 8.

O Child, most truly God's own Son,
O crib, O throne of Solomon,
O stall, O place of pure delight,
O straw, like roses red and white!
Infant in the stall, all our sins destroy!
Infant in the straw, give us joy!

O Child, most wonderful your birth,
Your gracious coming to our earth!
Milk-white, blood-red, your body gives
Fresh courage to our humble lives.
Chorus

Your hair is curly, gold your head,
Your eyes are clear, your lips are red,
Most beautiful, most honey-sweet
Your body is from head to feet.
Chorus

Like ivory your snow-white skin,
A glowing sapphire set therein,
The sapphire is the Godhead great,
The ivory your mortal state.
Chorus

Your hands are full of summer flowers
That smell more sweetly after showers;
You sparkle, Child, more beautiful
Than if the sun were in the stall.
Chorus

The Godhead lies within your breast
To grant the heart its chief request;
Heav'n has itself no greater grace
Than clearly shines in your sweet face.
Chorus

A Swiss traditional text to a seventeenth-century German melody form the basis of this carol. Written in 1979, Fred's words fit with Allen Percival's adaptation of the melody (INFANT IN THE STALL). It was commissioned for *The Galliard Book of Carols* and is included in a popular selection *32 Galliard Carols for Christmas*.

100 The Joy of Being Friends

7.6.7.6.

How rich is God's creation,
How varied all he made!
How wide a range of colour
Is everywhere displayed!

No two of us his children
Are truly born as twins;
The most alike will differ
In virtues and in sins.

Let none in scorn or envy
Another's right refuse;
But all delight to welcome
Each gift that God can use.

Before we hurt each other
In gaining our own ends,
God grant we may discover
The joy of being friends.

At the annual conference of the Methodist Church Music Society in 1979, Norman Coles mentioned that he would soon be speaking to the Women's Fellowship at The Drive Methodist Church, Sevenoaks, on the difference between men and women, under the title 'Vive la Difference', seeking to bring out the various ways in which God uses the attributes of both sexes. Surely, he asked, Fred must have a hymn on this theme tucked away somewhere? Fred's typical response was to offer to write one. The original version included the following final verse, which Norman felt summed up his talk:

> For God in love unites us—
> Not only husband, wife—
> But all who share together
> The mysteries of life.

The revision was made to respond to a request for texts for children's and young people's choir items from the Choristers' Guild in the United States whose aim is to build Christian character through singing. It could be a useful hymn at Harvest Festival, especially in urban areas, where thanksgiving for various talents is often part of the pattern of worship.

Possible tunes are: CHERRY TREE CAROL or EDMONDSHAM.

101 Faith Alive

6.6.6.6.8 8.

> Our fathers lived by faith,
> Set free from self and sin,
> By faith drove demons out,
> By faith drew outcasts in:
> And left the Church a heritage
> That shames a disbelieving age.

What godlessness destroys
Faith labours to restore;
Where doubt sees only change,
Faith finds an open door:
And all who come to Jesus prove
It's faith that makes the mountain move.

Then let us place ourselves
In God's creative hands,
Anchored in faith, but free
To do what he commands:
Not prisoners of our heritage
But born to serve the present age.

What need have we to wait
For others to advance,
For tides to turn, or folk
Be easier to convince?
The time is now, and he is ours,
With all his Spirit's mighty powers.

This hymn was written in 1979 for a series of Festivals of Praise in the East
Anglia District of the Methodist Church under the general title *Faith Alive*. It
was sung first at Downham Market in May 1980. The series ended with the
visit of the Methodist Conference to Norwich, when the Festival was held in
Norwich Cathedral on 9th July 1981. The tune chosen was MILLENIUM.

118

102 Easter Anticipated

8.8.8.8.8.6.

A Lenten Hymn

For forty days we mourn the day
When all creation held its breath,
When God in Man was done to death,
And hid his glory in our dust.
Until the stone was rolled away.
What was there left to trust?

For forty days we learn to share
The guilt of those who at the end
Failed, as we fail, their dying Friend,
And nursed their self-accusing woes.
They kept a vigil with despair
Until the sun arose.

In clearer light, these Lenten days,
We see the Christ upon his cross
In public wrongs and private loss,
In earthquake, famine, sickness, sword.
We wait for Easter's shout of praise:
He reigns, our risen Lord!

The Standing Commission on Church Music's Committee on Hymnal Revision of the Episcopal Church in the United States issued in January 1981 a list of areas needing texts as they plan their new hymnal. *Lent—anticipation of Easter* was one named gap to which Fred responded with this text. The other impetus was a tune GLASFRYN, written by Pam Barton, a Liverpool teacher of physically handicapped children, which Fred received in May 1981.

103 Christ Commits to Us

8 8 7.8 8 7.D.

**He is able to guard that which
I have committed unto him. (2 Timothy 1, 12 RV)
He is able to guard that which
he hath committed unto me. (RV margin)**

Lord, do you trust yourself to me?
Make me your own, yet leave me free
To follow or forsake you?
Then guard your life in me, I pray,
Lest I should drift or break away,
And my lost Saviour make you.
Without your help how can I steel
My will to overcome self-will,
Thus rise above temptation:
For well I know, yet do not know,
How secretly the pressures grow
That threaten our salvation.

Lord, do you trust your Church to me,
Its gospel, growth, integrity,
Its fellowship of loving?
Without your help how can I prove
To disbelieving minds that love
Is root of our believing?
So, Lord, when we resent the cross,
And in our failures love you less
Than when we are succeeding:
Put us to shame, defeat our pride;
Lord, bring us back to your dear side,
Saved by your interceding.

In a lecture on *English Hymnody: a look at some of the sources* (at the Oxford
International Hymnody Conference, 1981) John Wilson drew the attention
of the audience to the long history behind the tune known usually now as
PSALM 36 (68), suggesting it needed new words. Before the Conference
broke up, Fred wrote this hymn, refusing to be intimidated by the metre.

Other texts suitable for general use

Some offer God their busy hands **126**
One woman none could heal **127**
Where Temple offerings are made **129**
Praise her, as Jesus did! **130**
How many evils spoil our lives **131**
Here is one whose eager mind **134**
Two brothers came to blows **135**
Zacchaeus in the pay of Rome **137**
Lord Jesus, you were homeless **142**
How hard it was for them to stay **143**
On the road to Damascus, he's blinded by light **144**
Christ is preached in Caesarea **145**
When Father Abraham went out **147**
When Jesus walked by Galilee **149**
It may be they were Magi **150**
Who is it whistling on the hill **151**
When Jesus came preaching the Kingdom of God **158**
Nicodemus comes by night **159**
All of you share my gladness **161**
Blest be the King whose coming is in the name of God! **171**
All the sky is bright **173**
The night is nearly over **183**
By gracious powers so wonderfully sheltered **184**
This carol we gladly sing **185**
Angelic hosts proclaimed him, when he came, when he came **188**
How dark was the night of his coming! **189**
O Jesus Christ, as you awake **190**
Now, as we keep this famous fast **191**
Jesus, how strong is our desire **193**
Let my vision, Lord, be keen and clear this day; **198**

II

HYMNS
FOR
SPECIAL OCCASIONS

104 At a Civic Service

7.6.7.6.D.

Here, where past generations
Gave God the glory due,
Where wise men genuflected
Toward the good and true;
We too, in search of wisdom
For these decisive days,
Offer the God who made us
Our act of Christian praise.

How great the debt we owe them,
Those people of the past!
How many an honest craftsman
Created things that last!
Against what odds our fathers
Found courage to be free,
Our boundless skies above them,
And at their feet the sea!

By time's relentless justice
We shall in turn become
The former generation
Who made this land their home.
In truth may it be spoken
When our mistakes are plain:
They never sold the future
For quick or easy gain.

May God who calls us daily
To serve him here on earth,
Help us to find through worship
What is of lasting worth:
To end the sad dissensions
That wreck the good begun,
And seek no private heaven
Until his will is done.

This hymn was written for a Civic Service in 1974 at the request of Alan Webster, then Dean of Norwich, who has called it Fred's 'anti-inflation' hymn. Fred suggested KING'S LYNN as a tune, but the Cathedral organist chose WOLVERCOTE as better known. It was subsequently sung on several occasions in the Cathedral to THORNBURY.

  Incidentally, the local Norwich version of the text uses 'Anglian' rather than 'boundless' in the penultimate line of Verse 2.

105 On Hospital Sunday   8.6.8 8.6.

O God of all, our Servant God,
Within whose life we live,
Accept our praise and daily bless
In each vocation we profess
The service each would give.

How wise they were who long ago
In solemn vows conceived
Their calling as a trust, and strove
With less of science than of love
To act as they believed.

125

Grant us, with our maturer skills,
To have as strict a care:
From useless rituals set us free,
From all that blunts efficiency
And mars the work we share.

In every longed-for new advance,
Lest those we help be harmed,
Hold us, in hope, to our intent,
But keep us, through experiment,
Far-sighted and forearmed.

And grant to those we seek to heal,
Whose lives are in our hands,
A stronger faith than we can give,
And that instinctive will to live
On which our skills depends.

This hymn was written at the request of Erik Routley when he was Minister of St. James' Congregational Church, Newcastle-upon-Tyne for use at a service on St. Luke's Day 1969 where it was sung to REPTON. Later Francis Westbrook wrote the tune OAKLEIGH PARK for it, and this was printed in *26 Hymns*.

106 Christian Aid

7.6.7.6.D.
(Trochaic)

Once upon a time they went,
King and page together,
On a deed of kindness bent,
In the winter weather.
Every legend has its truth,
May this one remind us
Where a neighbour is in need
Christ expects to find us.

Victims of injustice cry:
On your own confession
Charity is not enough,
We must end oppression.
Yet, in such a world as this,
Daily we are proving
There are evils none can cure
Without deeds of loving.

We must follow in his steps
Who was found in fashion
As a man, yet never lost
His divine compassion.
Lord, release such love in us
We shall be more ready
To reach out with speedy aid
To your poor and needy.

In 1977, Fred received from Dorothy Bartholomew, Chairman of the Christian Aid Commission of Norwich Council of Churches, a request for a hymn or song for a Christian Aid Youth Event in Norwich Cathedral the following year. After a draft or two, Fred came up with this hymn to be sung to the tune for which Neale wrote his famous carol *Good King Wenceslas*, which could be called a Victorian Christian Aid song. The hymn was later published in the all-age hymn-book *Partners in Praise*, and then appeared in *The Galliard Book of Carols* alongside both the Latin text and a modern version of the ancient Spring carol TEMPUS ADEST FLORIDUM, the melody in *Piae Cantiones* (1582) giving us the well-known tune.

107 For a Christmas Gift Service

7.5.7.5.
and Chorus

Jesus is God's gift to us
Born on Christmas Day.
How we love to think of him
Sleeping in the hay!
The calf said MOO!
And the lamb said BAA!
And the donkey stamped his feet;
And Joseph said HUSH!
And Mary smiled
As Kings and Shepherds hurried to greet
The Christ Child!
The Christ Child!
The Christ Child!

This is why on Christmas Day
Gifts are on the tree.
This is why I love to give,
And others give to me.
Chorus

Jesus is God's gift to us,
This and every day,
How we love to think of him
Sleeping in the hay!
Chorus

This carol was written for occasions when young children give gifts to other children. Complete with a tune THORPE GREEN Fred wrote himself, it contained the directive, 'The children will *Moo!* and *Baa!* and say *Hush!* with their fingers on their lips, and even stamp their feet!' It was slightly revised and printed in 1979 in *Partners in Praise* with the tune STABLE which has a tongue-in-cheek flavour in its use of an otherwise familiar musical phrase. This tune omits the repetitions of 'The Christ Child' in the chorus.

108 For a Toy Service

We haven't come from far,
Like wise men did of old;
We can't bring Jesus myrrh,
Or frankincense, or gold:
* *But here's a bouncing ball,*
And here's a box of bricks,
And here's a woolly toy,
So every child can enjoy
Christmas!
Christmas!
Christmas!

We've come from very near,
Like shepherds did of old;
But we haven't got a fleece
For Jesus, if he's cold:
Chorus

* It is intended that other gifts shall be named to suit the circumstances.

This simple carol was written following a request from the Primary Leader of St. Mark's Methodist Church, Cheltenham, where it was used in 1972. Francis Westbrook set it a little later to a charming, unpublished tune LITHERLAND. The Music Editors of *Partners in Praise* selected an arrangement of a nursery rhyme melody by Allen Percival when it was chosen for this Family Worship selection in 1979. This version CHRISTMAS BOX provides for three loud claps in the chorus before a single 'Christmas!' Fred notes there should be lots of excitement at the end of the chorus.

109 Carol for a Christingle Service 12.11.12.11.

O round as the world is the orange you give us!
And happy are they who to Jesus belong:
So let the world know, as we join in Christingle,
That Jesus, the Hope of the World, is our song.

O bright is the flame of the candle you give us!
And happy are they who to Jesus belong:
So let the world know, as we join in Christingle,
That Jesus, the Light of the World, is our song.

Go northward or southward, go eastward or westward,
How happy are they who to Jesus belong!
So let the world know, as they join in Christingle,
That Jesus, the Peace of the World, is our song.

When homeward we go, we must take Jesus with us,
For happy are they who to Jesus belong:
So let the world know, as we join in Christingle,
That Jesus, the Saviour of all, is our song.

Fred's wife Marjorie has for some years served as a guide in Norwich
Cathedral and, in 1979, thus met a Mr and Mrs Fillingham of Sheffield.
Discovering that Marjorie's husband was a hymn-writer, they wondered if he
would write something for a Christingle Service. (Mrs Fillingham is a local
secretary of the Church of England Children's Society.) Fred had never
heard of 'Christingle'—though it is celebrated as near home as the Cathedral
itself—but soon he had found out all about the ancient custom and wrote this
hymn for it.

Allen Percival, one of the editors of *The Galliard Book of Carols*,
suggested a traditional Czech tune, now christened CHRISTINGLE. The
hymn is also published in *32 Galliard Carols for Christmas*.

110 For Parade Services

5.5.5.4.D.

Let us all praise him,
God our Creator,
Who in our Scouting*
Makes us all one:
Shares our adventures,
Strengthens our friendships,
Asks of us service,
Faithfully done.

Badge of achievement,
Win it and wear it!
Living is learning
All our life long.
Some find it easy,
Some find it harder:
Each makes the other
Proud to belong.

Let us all praise him,
God of all nations,
Seeking in worship
What is of worth:
Serving our country,
Living as neighbours,
Offering friendship
Wide as the earth.

* or Movement.

© For permission to reproduce this text, see page 239.

This hymn was originally written for a presentation to Queen's Guides of the 11th Norwich Company at Bowthorpe Road Methodist Church, Norwich. The Scout Association willingly accepted it for use in their Movement. It could prove relevant to other uniformed organisations. The tune is BUNESSAN.

131

111 For a Sports Service

8.6.8.6.D.
(D.C.M.)

As athletes gather round the track,
Or players take the field,
There's not an honest sport but claims
The best that each can yield.
With body fit and mind alert,
And spirit disciplined,
We beat fatigue and fight it out,
And get our second wind.

Let all the fans go mad with joy
If victory comes their way;
And staid spectators rise to greet
The hero of the day:
But whether it was won or lost,
May everyone agree
It was the game that mattered most,
And not the victory.

Our life itself is like a race,
The great apostle said—
The game of games we all must play
For more than daily bread.
Whatever spells true happiness
Let none of us destroy,
For God has given us all these things
Most richly to enjoy.

The original version was written in response to a request, made in 1979 by Hubert Julian, Organist and Choirmaster of Newquay Wesley Church, for a hymn for use in their Junior Church Anniversary service which had 'Sport' as its theme. The day after receiving the request Fred was staying in Sevenoaks. As soon as the first draft was completed, it was hastily duplicated and tried out by The Drive Methodist Church Choir that very evening. The version above is a little more generalised than the original. Suggested tunes are THE FLIGHT OF THE EARLS or TYROL.

112 For a Flower Festival in Westminster Abbey

7.6.7.6.D.
(Trochaic)

Praise the Lord for all delights;
Praise the world's Creator!
Who shall say of sounds and sights
Which joy is the greater?
Offer him these gifts of ours,
All our art's continuing:
Deck the Abbey Church with flowers,
Flowers of his own giving.

Long before God gave us birth—
We or any creature—
Flowers adorned the naked earth,
Changed the face of nature.
Tended now by hands of ours,
See how they are thriving!
Deck the Abbey Church with flowers:
They are our thanksgiving.

God it is who gives us bread.
God who gives us beauty;
God it is who for our good
Lays on us this duty—
Earth is his, and earth is ours,
Given to us for sharing;
Share the Master's love of flowers,
Share his work of caring.

133

Here in pageantries of State
Speaks a free-born nation:
Here, in Christ, we celebrate
Fullness of salvation.
Deck the Abbey Church with flowers,
Certain, though they perish,
What God gives, for ever ours,
We must learn to cherish.

This hymn was commissioned by Alan Luff, Precentor and Sacrist of Westminster Abbey, for the great Flower Festival there in June 1981 organised by the National Association of Flower Arrangement Societies of Great Britain. The whole of the Abbey (including the Royal Chapels, the Cloisters and the Chapel House) was decked with over 300 displays associated with its history and that of the City of London Guilds. Fred submitted two hymns, this one especially written for the occasion, and another (see **113**). It was meant for the tune TEMPUS ADEST FLORIDUM (The time of flowers is here), to which *Good King Wenceslas* is commonly sung, as being one of the best-known tunes to church-goers and non church-goers alike.

113 At a Festival of Flowers   6.6.6.6.8 8.

Sing praises, one and all,
Who for a few brief hours
Share in this Festival
The Master's love of flowers.
Let Nature, hand-in-hand with Art,
Amaze our eyes and warm our heart.

How long it took to form
The wild flowers at our feet!
What ravages of storm,
What stress of cold and heat!
By Nature taught, how patient those
Who learned to cultivate a rose!

Westminster Abbey, with Farringtons School Choir (see **12**)

At work in Norwich

John Wilson (see **1**)

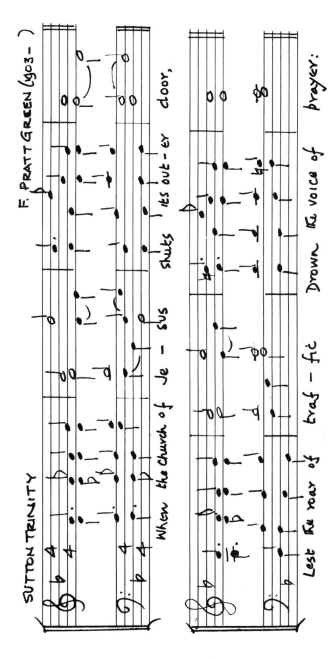

The opening of Fred's own tune SUTTON TRINITY, in his autograph.

Outside St. Paul's Cathedral, London.

So take what Nature gives
With awe and gratitude:
For everything that lives,
Its purpose understood,
Is part of that mysterious whole
In which we glimpse the beautiful.

Believing we are free
To serve God's great design,
We cry, 'He cares for me,
And makes his purpose mine'.
Here, in this Festival of Flowers,
Rejoice that such a life is ours!

This is the third version of the hymn for Flower Festivals. Written first for a local occasion at the request of Philip Carter, organist and choirmaster of Totterdown Methodist Church, Bristol, it was amended for Westminster Abbey's Flower Festival of 1981 and submitted with the preceding hymn, which was the one chosen. It was nevertheless sung in the version above in the Abbey in a *Come and Sing* session in May 1981 with the additional verse specially written for the Abbey, and used shortly afterwards for a flower festival at Petersfield, Hampshire. The tune suggested is EASTVIEW by Vernon Lee.

114 The Bells of St. Paul's   8 8.8 8.8 8.

When ringers in full circle stand,
A peal of bells at their command,
What skill and discipline is theirs
To call a nation to its prayers.
Come, come to me! our Saviour calls:
Come to him! say the Bells of St. Paul's!

In times of triumph, times of loss,
The bells ring out beneath the cross;
In joyous or in solemn sound
They raise our spirits from the ground.
Come, come to me! our Saviour calls:
Come to him! say the Bells of St. Paul's!

God bless the ringers as they swing
The mighty bells to make them ring,
And God bless all who hear their tongues
Proclaims to whom the world belongs.
Come, come to me! our Saviour calls:
Come to him! say the Bells of St. Paul's.

The version printed here is as shown in *The Galliard Book of Carols.* The original was written for Evensong at St. Paul's Cathedral, London, commemorating the centenary in 1978 of the dedication of the cathedral bells. The Service was attended by the St. Paul's Cathedral Guild of Ringers and other members of the Ancient Society of College Youths and by a congregation of bell-ringers from far and near. There was an extra verse between the last two printed here:

Above the office blocks and banks,
The shops and ships, the bells give thanks
For all that Mother Church has taught,
For our redemption, dearly bought.
Come, come to me! our Saviour calls:
Come to him! say the Bells of St. Paul's.

The tune was Vaughan Williams' arrangement of SUSSEX CAROL. The text was also reproduced in *The Ringing World*, the official journal of the Central Council of Church Bell-ringers.

115 We Ring the Earth with Praise   6.6.6.6.8 8.

Come, celebrate with us
The few who, met in prayer,
Confessed their sinfulness,
And knew what they must share:
Their faith that it is Christ alone
Redeems the world, and makes it one.

They set apart one day,
In each succeeding year,
And called on us to pray,
And on our conscience bear
Our stricken world that needs to find
In God new hope for humankind.

Christ's body by its scars
Warns us how hard our task;
No magic rules the stars,
Or gives us what we ask.
Yet prayer, they knew, has power to move
Whatever thwarts a work of love.

So, drawn from every race,
We ring the earth with praise,
Each in our time and place,
And our accustomed ways:
And offer God, in all our lands,
Our thankful hearts and willing hands.

Then let our song of joy
All other music drown,
And praise itself employ
A language all its own:
To God, whom heaven and earth adore,
Be glory now, and evermore!

This hymn was commissioned by the National Committee for England,
Wales and Northern Ireland of the Women's World Day of Prayer for use at
their Golden Jubilee celebrations in 1982 in the Royal Albert Hall, London.
At the same time, Fred received from Valerie Ruddle the tune TRAVAIL (see
91) on which he worked with *Come, celebrate with us* in mind. It was however
unsuitable for a festive occasion and Valerie subsequently wrote ATLANTIC
BRIDGE.

116 At the Dedication of a Church C.M.

AT THE DEDICATION OF THE CHURCH

We enter, Lord, and are at home
Already in your house.
May we, by knowing why we come,
Put it to Christian use.

AT THE FONT

Here, Lord, the newly-born receive
Into your earthly fold,
That, growing up, we may believe,
And rest in you when old.

AT THE PULPIT AND LECTERN

Here shall your living Word be read,
Interpreted and taught;
So we, by your wise Spirit led,
May serve you as we ought.

AT THE LORD'S TABLE

> Here has your Cross a central place
> In sacrament and sign;
> Here we shall meet you face to face
> In broken bread and wine.

AT THE ORGAN, STAINED-GLASS WINDOW, ETC.

> And here shall art, inspired by you
> In what we hear and see,
> Help us to understand the true,
> Yet keep its mystery.

AT THE DEDICATION OF THE PEOPLE

> Your consecrated people now,
> Lord, cleanse us from our sins,
> That endless good may ever flow
> From what this day begins.

Fred's speed at getting down to commissions is highlighted here in a scrapbook note:

> Requested 10th January 1973 by Rev. Norman Pickering of
> Bowes Park for opening of new church. Written next day.

His first draft was mulled over by Norman Pickering, his ministerial colleague Brian Tebbutt, and a working group which led to some correspondence during which Fred wrote saying his approach to hymn-writing was professional—he welcomed discussion to get the thing right as an architect is ready to talk about his plans and modify them, if this is desirable.

The following extract from one of Norman Pickering's letters is significant in expressing the mood of thinking in 1973. It concerns the use of 'house' in the first verse.

> We have our definite reservations about ideas of the 'sacredness'
> of the 'House of God'. In the present climate, this Solomonic
> approach to church architecture is something to be played down
> rather than brought to the fore. Is God present in a special way in
> the environment of a church building? Does such a building
> enjoy a higher concentration of deity than others? Clearly there
> is heavy support through many years for 'House of God' type
> vocabulary, but isn't the need just now for another emphasis to
> counter-balance that one? The false division between the sacred
> and the secular is still very prevalent....

The original intention was that the hymn should be sung to AMAZING GRACE but LONDON NEW was used at the service at Trinity-at-Bowes in Palmers Green, North London, on 21st July 1973.

139

117 For a Centenary Celebration 8 8 8. and Alleluias

A hundred years! How small a part
Of Christian time for us to chart!
How much to stir the thankful heart!
Alleluia!

Here generations, face to face
With Christ, enjoyed renewing grace.
And made of this a sacred place.
Alleluia!

The older vision fades and dies;
A new world greets our anxious eyes:
The same Lord leads our enterprise.
Alleluia!

Forgetting what is past, said Paul,
Let us press on towards the goal
Which Christ has set before us all.
Alleluia!

In changing times, how hard to see
What our next step of faith must be:
Lord, make it clear to us—and me!

Note: No Alleluia is sung at the end of the last verse.

This hymn in its original form was for the centenary celebration of St. Paul's Methodist Church, Didsbury, the 'college chapel' when Fred was a student there. This revision is to make it suitable for any centenary celebration. The tune is VULPIUS (GELOBT SEI GOTT). The omission of the *Alleluia* from the last verse is dramatically effective.

140

118 A Hymn in Celebration of Fifty Years of Methodist Union

8 8.6.D.

How good it is when we agree
To live in Christian unity,
Fulfilling Christ's command;
When, putting prejudice aside,
Superior status, injured pride,
We take the outstretched hand.

Time was, we found it hard to greet
Those other saints across the street
Who bore our tribal name.
Divided then, one people now,
What have these fifty years to show,
What progress dare we claim?

So little done, so far to go!
Yet God has given us grace to grow
In love that makes us one:
And strengthened our resolve to see
Christ's Church renewed in unity,
And serving him alone.

For all these signs of hope we raise
Our voices in a hymn of praise
Outsoaring every song:
And worship him, the God of love,
In whom all creatures live and move,
To whom all souls belong.

The Methodist Conference of 1982, meeting in Plymouth, celebrates the fiftieth anniversary of Methodist Union. The Editor of the Conference Handbook asked Fred for the words and commissioned the tune POLWHELE from Hubert Julian, Secretary of the Cornwall Methodist District Music Committee.

141

119 For a Golden Jubilee

How right that we should offer
To God unceasing praise,
Yet mark the church's seasons,
Her high and holy days:
Then share with us this story
We would not leave untold—
Our fifty years of learning
To be Christ's flock and fold.

Through years of disillusion,
Of threatened liberty,
When dawns brought little prospect
Of better things to be,
God's servants came together
To meet a people's needs,
Whose names we justly honour,
Their foresight and their deeds.

What they and we accomplish
We frankly would recite;
Alike success and failure
Set down in black and white:
Yet this is hidden from us,
For none but God can trace
How much is our achievement,
How much a work of grace.

Who can foretell the future,
What claims we must obey?
We pray we may not face it
Our faith in disarray.
Lord God, revealed in Jesus,
Your Church, and us, endow
With wisdom, love, and courage
To serve your Kingdom now.

© 1982. For permission to reproduce this text, see page ii.

This hymn for the tune JUBILATE was especially written for the Golden Jubilee in May 1981 of Shirley Methodist Church on the Southern outskirts of London, where Fred served as Minister in the nineteen-fifties. The revised version above is intended for churches celebrating their golden jubilee in the next decade.

120 Our Heritage in Christ

14.14.14.14.
and Chorus L.M.

How great our debt to pioneers, who in our nation's youth
Had Bibles in their work-worn hands, its precepts in their hearts,
Who built their meeting houses, unadorned, as gospel truth,
To be a home for sinners, where a new life truly starts.
Then let us bind ourselves this day
To live for Christ, as bold as they
In simple, humble faith to claim:
We are his Church, we bear his Name.

The nation prospered, grew apace, a people on the move,
Who grasped at opportunities, had freedom to defend,
Who saw their gathered churches as communities of love,
Committed to the Lord of Life, whose Kingdom has no end.
Then let us bind ourselves this day
To live for Christ, as proud as they,
In hymn and liturgy to claim:
We are his Church, we bear his Name.

This heritage in Christ is ours, a mission to fulfil:
How impotent our churches are without his power and grace!
The future is an open door Christ sets before us still,
The door of his compassion for our needy human race.
Then let us bind ourselves this day
To live for Christ, as proud as they,
And prove by deeds our right to claim:
We are his Church, we bear his Name.

This hymn is essentially for the New World! It was commissioned for the 125th Anniversary of the First Presbyterian Church, Arlington Heights, Chicago, Illinois. Austin Lovelace was commissioned to provide an anthem setting, which is published by Belwin-Mills Publishing Corporation for wider use.

121 At a Celebration of the Restoration of a Church

8 8 8. and Alleluias

Now God be praised, the work is done!
This was their cry in centuries gone,
Who built our churches, stone by stone:
Alleluia!

What Time disfigured, turned to dust,
We have renewed, as Christians must
Who hold faith's heritage in trust:
Alleluia!

Now, to God's glory, we must prove
This is the base from which we move
To do his waiting tasks of love:
Alleluia!

So may the living Church, restored
In mind and spirit by her Lord,
Not only speak but live his word:
Alleluia!

Most Holy, Undivided Three,
Use us to build, in unity,
Your church, as you would have her be:
Alleluia!

Fred's tenth scrapbook contains the Order of Service for an Act of Thanksgiving for the restoration of the Cathedral Church of the Holy and Undivided Trinity of Norwich in the presence of Her Majesty the Queen on 11th April 1975. In the version sung the second and third lines read:

This was their cry who, centuries gone,
Built this cathedral, stone by stone:

The tune used was VULPIUS (GELOBT SEI GOTT).

122 At the Dedication of an Organ

7.6.7.6.D.
(Trochaic)

What a joy it is to sing
When the Spirit moves us!
There's no gift we cannot bring
To the God who loves us.
Every instrument is blest
If for him we use it;
When he asks of us our best,
How can we refuse it?

Voluntaries, anthems, chants,
Hymns of every metre:
Who shall say which instruments
Serve our purpose better?
Here the organ is our choice,
Versatile yet simple:
Dedicate it—and rejoice
God is in his temple.

God is our tremendous theme,
Father, Son and Spirit;
He shall guard our faith in him,
Teach us how to share it.
Then in worship we shall find
Strength and consolation,
Greater love for humankind,
Depth of adoration.

This hymn was written as the request of Methodist Minister Bryan Spinney, for the dedication of an organ at his Bristol church in 1981. Fred discovered in *The Hymn-Book of the Church of England in Canada* (1938) an early tune by Arthur Sullivan ST. KEVIN which charmed him—and the organist concerned.

123 In Honour of St. Ninian

8.6.8.6.D.
(D.C.M.)

Before the Legions marched away
And chaos darkened all,
The Lord sent Ninian back to us,
With gospel fire, from Gaul.
Though much is buried deep in time,
And much has been outgrown,
Today we meet to celebrate
This saint who is our own.

For here, in Scotland, Ninian built
His Mission Church of stone,
And cells as white as purity
For those who pray alone.
And here he trained evangelists,
And sent them far and wide—
None knows how great their sacrifice,
Save him, the Crucified.

The facts and mysteries of faith
That drove Saint Ninian on,
Sustain us still, in heart and will,
And make all Christians one.
May we defeat, as he did then,
Those dark satanic powers
That war against the souls of men,
And daily threaten ours.

146

Say not that Ninian toiled in vain,
That all he gained was lost;
The Light is never overcome,
Though skies be overcast.
In fellowship with all the saints
Take courage from the past;
Before us lies eternity,
And Christ shall reign at last!

Little did those who wrote in 1977 from Whithorn in the extreme South-West of Scotland to ask for a hymn in honour of Saint Ninian know it was a favourite holiday spot for Fred! He heard the hymn sung on 11th June 1978 at Morning Service in the Priory Church, Whithorn in practice for the Open-Air celebration in the Priory Ruins in July that year. Suggested tunes are PETERSHAM or FOREST GREEN.

124 In Honour of St. Boniface   L.M.

We honour, one in Christ, this day
A Wessex child who grew in grace,
A monk no hindrance could dismay:
This saint we gave the German race.

A cloistered life of active prayer
Was not for him, though truly blest:
His love of Jesus led him where,
In Fresia, he would serve him best.

From all, except obedience, freed,
He preached to all the word of grace:
And churches lax in life and creed,
Learned discipline from Boniface.

147

In great events he played his part,
Princes and Popes gave him their trust:
But simple virtues warmed his heart,
And worldly pomp he counted dust.

At last, in Fresia, where his own
To save him would have fought and died,
He offered Christ his martyr's crown,
True servant of the Crucified.

Lord, grant us strength in unity,
For mission in the Spirit's might,
And send your Church such saints as he
To lead all nations to the light.

This hymn was written for the 1300th anniversary of the birth of the great Apostle to the Germans, St. Boniface. The Rev. Amos Creswell, the Chairman of the Plymouth and Exeter District of the Methodist Church commended Fred as a possible hymn-writer to the Rev. Bruce Duncan, Vicar of Crediton, who needed the hymn for a Festival Service to be held in the Collegiate Church of the Holy Cross, Crediton, to celebrate the birth of their saint in the town long centuries ago. It was sung (with a minor amendment in verse 1, suitable for the special occasion) to FULDA on 5th June 1980. The Bishop of Crediton supplied a wise revision incorporated in the final version of verse 2.

Other suggested tunes are VERBUM SUPERNUM, EISENACH and GONFALON ROYAL.

125 In Commemoration of Julian of Norwich

10 10.11 11. or
5 5.5 5.6 5.6 5.
(Anapaestic)

Rejoice in God's saints
This day of all days!
A world without saints
Forgets how to praise!
Rejoice in their courage,
Their spiritual skill;
In Julian of Norwich
Rejoice, all who will!

148

The candle she lit
Six centuries gone,
By darkness beset
Shines quietly on.
Her cell is no prison,
Though narrow and dim,
For Jesus is risen,
And she lives in him.

How bright in her cell
The showings of God!
No writings could tell
What love understood.
She suffers his Passion,
She grieves over sin;
She knows his compassion
Has made us all kin.

How courteous is God!
All love and all light!
In God's Motherhood
She finds her delight.
She pleads for the sinner,
She wrestles with Hell;
God answers: *All manner
Of things shall be well!*

Dear Lord, we would learn
To walk in this way,
With patience discern
How best to obey
That call to perfection
You taught us to face:
Lord, fix our direction,
And keep us in grace.

This was one of two hymns written for the 600th Anniversary of *Relevations of Divine Love*. It was sung at the beginning of an ecumenical Eucharist at Norwich Cathedral on 5th May 1973 to the tune LAUDATE DOMINUM. The other hymn, which ended the service has taken on a wider life in a revised form (see **52**).

The hymn printed above continues to be sung in Julian circles.

III

BALLADS

Within this section are texts of religious significance which tell stories and one or two protest songs. The word we have chosen to describe these is 'ballad'. These scripts, except in borderline circumstances, would not generally be considered as hymns though most could properly be sung within the context of worship, sometimes as a solo or by a choir or group rather than by a congregation.

Texts Commissioned by Lee Hastings Bristol, Jnr.

The late Lee Hastings Bristol, Jnr., a member of the Episcopal Church of America, well-known in the United States as a person who combined the arts of preaching and music making, commissioned Fred to write texts for his radio work and for special preaching assignments. Without Lee's encouragement and sponsorship, these ballads would never have been written.

They form three groups. Printed first is a group on Women of the Gospels (**126** to **132**). These are followed by ballads relating mostly to men of the New Testament (**133** to **141**). The final group is based round cities, ancient and modern (**142** to **146**). With one or two exceptions, they were to be sung to his own simple and attractive tunes.

126 Martha and Mary

C.M.

Some offer God their busy hands,
And some a quiet heart;
What Jesus graciously defends
Is Mary's better part.

A supper worthy of their Guest
Is Martha's chief concern;
That Mary understands him best
Is hard for her to learn.

She falls into a fretful mood,
And sharply speaks her mind,
Forgetful that the body's food
Is not the only kind.

She earns how gentle a rebuke;
A woman not unblest,
Who in her eagerness mistook
The good for what is best.

Teach us to serve, yet never cease
To listen, Lord, to you,
And in your presence be at peace
When we have most to do.

© For permission to reproduce this text, see page 239.

127 The Woman who touched the Hem of his Garment

6.6.6.6.

One woman none could heal,
To touch him, if she could,
Pressed forward in the crowd
To where the Master stood.

Who touched me? Jesus said:
The question seemed absurd:
In such a crowd as this
How many touched the Lord!

But she, so great her faith,
At last had found release;
Trembling, she told him all,
And won his 'Go in peace!'

Lord, by your presence heal
Our sickness and our shame,
Though all we dare to do
Is touch your garment's hem.

128 The Woman taken in Adultery

She stood, her guilt laid bare
By heartless men, a snare
To trap the Sinners' Friend,
Who either must approve
Her death by stoning or defend
The lust that some call love.

You did not raise your head
But wrote in sand; and said:
'Let him who has no sin
Be first to cast a stone'—
And there was none who dared begin,
Of all the righteous, none!

Yet when they all had gone
You did not, Lord, condone
The sin that was her shame,
But bade her sin no more.
O love of God, so slow to blame,
So eager to restore!

© For permission to reproduce this text, see page 239.

129 The Widow's Mite   C.M.

Where Temple offerings are made,
And knowing he must die,
Our Master, resting in the shade,
Watches the world go by.

Some offer silver, others gold,
Some what they can afford;
Some give, in order to withhold,
And some to gain reward.

Nameless as shadows on a wall
The poorer come and go;
It is as if he knows them all,
As only God can know.

A widow, passing by, who scarce
Can scrape enough to live,
Finding two pennies in her purse
Gives all that she can give.

How deeply moved he is by this
He leaves us in no doubt:
And he himself will die for us,
Before the week is out.

130 The Woman who Anointed Christ   6.6.6.6.6.6.

Praise her, as Jesus did!
For it was she who read
The suffering in his face,
What darkness lay ahead,
Her Lord defamed, betrayed,
His body cold and dead.

The costly oil she kept
For some half-dreamed of use,
She poured out as a gift,
Which, though it earned abuse
From some who called it waste,
With fragrance filled the house.

Let reason work things out,
And wisely count the cost!
Love is dissatisfied
With less that uttermost,
And knows that nothing given
To him is ever lost.

So thank the Lord of Love
For love's extravagance!
In that he gave himself
For every sinner once,
He shows us love alone
Shall, at the last, convince.

155

131 Mary Magdalene

8.8.8.8.8 8.

How many evils spoil our lives,
An end to what we might have been!
Our demons vex us, drag us down,
Until, like Mary Magdalene,
We meet, on some God-given day
You, whom all demons must obey.

Mighty is your transforming love!
You drove her seven demons out,
Freed her from infirmities,
And in a dawn of grief and doubt
Called her by name, and at a word
Became again her living Lord.

May you, the Risen Christ, perform
In each of us your work of grace;
By transplant, most miraculous,
And, to our endless joy, replace
This dying self, with its desires,
By that new self your love inspires.

132 The Woman of Samaria

L.M.

She went alone to Jacob's Well,
At noon, when nobody would stare,
Surprised to find a stranger there
And he a Jew as she could tell.

When Jesus offered her a drink,
That would forever quench her thirst,
She made a joke of it at first,
Not knowing what to say or think.

From prophets nothing can be hid;
One word was quite enough to show
There was not much he did not know,
He told her all she ever did.

Is this Messiah? Come and see!
Her challenge is effective still:
And any place is Jacob's Well
Where Christ encounters you and me.

133 The Man at the Pool of Bethesda

How crowded the Pool of Bethesda
As sick and spectators awaited
The angel who troubled the waters;
How frantic the struggle for healing,
How often, how cruelly fated,
The man who had no one to help him!

Say not, 'I have no one to help me',
As long as the Friend of the Friendless
Stands by you to share your affliction;
For last shall be first in his Kingdom,
Whose power and compassion are endless.
Come quickly, Lord Jesus, and heal us!

134 The Rich Young Ruler

7 7.7 7.

Here is one whose eager mind
Wants, beyond all doubt, to find
Life's essential blessedness,
What is lasting, nothing less.

Young and rich, he comes to you,
Asking what he ought to do.
Yes, from boyhood he has sought
To observe what Moses taught.

For the sake of such a youth.
Make it easy, trim the truth!
All or nothing, it must be—
'Travel light, and follow me!'

Sad at heart, you let him go.
Must the answer, then, be 'no'?
Shall I also walk away?
Lord, I come, and come to stay!

135 The Man who wanted his Brother to divide the Inheritance

S.M.

Two brothers come to blows
On what is rightly theirs:
One wants the whole inheritance,
The other equal shares.

'Lord, make my brother share!'
The thwarted brother pleads;
And it is plain for all to see
What discord money breeds.

The answer Jesus gives
Let no one take amiss:
'I did not come to arbitrate
In such a case as this.'

But what he came to do
Is plain for all to heed:
He comes to save us from ourselves,
Our jealousy and greed.

136 The Man born Blind   L.M.

He healed the darkness of my mind
The day he gave my sight to me:
It was not sin that made me blind;
It was no sinner made me see.

Let others call my faith a lie,
Or try to stir up doubt in me:
Look at me now! None can deny
I once was blind and now I see!

Ask me not how! But I know who
Has opened up new worlds to me:
This Jesus does what none can do—
I once was blind, and now I see.

137 Zacchaeus

C.M.

Zacchaeus in the pay of Rome
Is climbing up a tree;
He wants to see a holy man—
The Man from Galilee.

The holy man is looking up,
Zacchaeus looking down:
'Zacchaeus, I must dine with you,
Before I leave the town!'

Zacchaeus, Son of Abraham,
Is overcome with shame:
For he who eats with holy men
Will never be the same.

Zacchaeus is a happy man,
A man new-born is he!
But Jesus takes the road again,
To die upon a Tree.

© For permission to reproduce this text, see page 239.

138 Pilate

What sort of man did Pilate see,
Standing his trial, God knows why:
What sort of man was he?
A tragic victim of human hate?
A crank who might imperil the State?
A man to be flogged and then set free,
Or a man he would have to crucify?
Jesus, my Jesus, doomed to die!
What sort of man was he?
Jesus, what sort of man was he?

What sort of man did Jesus see,
Sitting in judgement, God knows why,
What sort of man was he?
A man tight-cornered by human hate?
A man afraid to imperil the State?
A man to whom truth was expediency,
Who would yield when they shouted 'Crucify!'?
Jesus, my Jesus, doomed to die!
What sort of man was he,
Pilate, what sort of man was he?

Who was on trial that judgement day,
Jesus or Pilate, would you say?
Who was on trial that judgement day?

139 The Penitent Thief

What are they: freedom fighters, common thieves,
These sharers of Christ's agony and shame?
One taunts him cruelly, the other grieves
For him, perceiving he is free from blame,
And at the last believes.

See how the Christ, upon his cross, divides
Brother from brother, as he said he must:
For what he is compels us to take sides,
So one rejects, the other learns to trust:
One worships, one derides.

'Lord, when your kingdom comes, remember me!'
One cries, in penitence, and pays the price
That life exacts from such a man as he,
And, dying, is with Christ in paradise,
By saving grace set free.

140 Fasting and Feasting

It shocked them that the Master did not fast;
But Jesus wittily defends
A way of life less stern than John's:
Fasting would ill become the Bridegroom's friends.

How short a time for such festivity!
Soon they must mourn a Bridegroom slain,
And, fasting, share his suffering.
Then, one momentous morning, feast again!

Fasting and feasting, there is room for each:
But, Lord, let not our fasting strip
Our souls of joy, or feasting blunt
The disciplines of our discipleship.

141 Would-Be Disciples

Of the many who flocked to hear you,
Some hung on your every word,
Were eager to call you 'Lord':
You knew them, your would-be disciples.

To one who made easy promises
'The Son of Man', you said,
'Has nowhere to lay his head';
To the timid you gave encouragement.

But the man who procrastinated
You warned against looking back.
You, Lord, know what I lack:
Make me fit for the Kingdom of God.

142 Bethlehem

7.6.7.6.

Lord Jesus, you were homeless
The night you came to earth,
No hands prepared your cradle,
No fire lit up the hearth.

You made the stable homely,
And Mary doubly blest,
By crying for her comfort,
And feeding at her breast.

For every place is homely
Where love has done its best,
Though our misfortunes put us
Among the dispossessed.

Child by your incarnation,
Make them our special care;
And be yourself our refuge
In shelterless despair.

For no one shall be homeless
Who finds at Bethlehem
That God's eternal dwelling
Is open house to them.

143 Jerusalem

8.8.8.8.8 6.

How hard it was for them to stay,
Those followers of the Crucified:
To walk where once they ran away,
To see the hill where he had died.
Now Jesus lived, they longed to be
Safe home in Galilee.

But no! the Master's word was clear:
They must await their Pentecost
Not there, in Galilee, but here,
Where Jesus lived, where all was lost;
And here, where they had run away,
Proclaim the Promised Day.

Lord, when we also turn away
From all remembrance of our grief,
You, in your mercy, bid us stay,
To find, in courage, true relief,
Believing you will show us how
We best may serve you now.

Our Pentecosts are where we are!
Here where we yielded to defeat,
Where resurrection cures despair,
God's Spirit never fails to meet
Those who are anxious to receive
What God alone can give.

144 Damascus   Irregular

On the road to Damascus, he's blinded by light,
And falls to the ground
Like a man with a wound;
As love overwhelms him, he yields without fight.

You Christians in hiding, did none of you guess
What Jesus would do?
The incredible's true:
Saul came to arrest you; he's staying to bless!

He lodges awhile in the street you call Strait,
To grasp beyond doubt
What the gospel's about:
Whether Gentile or Jew, not one sinner need wait.

He offers Christ's peace, this apostle of strife;
And mighty the word
Of the crucified Lord,
Who is changing a world when he changes a life.

By our different ways may we reach the same place;
Be turned in our track,
And yet never go back
On the road to Damascus, God's Highway of Grace.

This text already existed, and had been sung to a somewhat extended arrangement of ARDWICK at the Hymn Society's Act of Praise in 1976 with the first line:

> As love speaks his name, and blinded by light

before Lee Hastings Bristol, Jnr. asked to use it in his 'Cities' Series. At that time, small changes were made to fit the melody the composer had in mind: this is now the accepted version.

145 Caesarea Maritima

8.7.8.7.
(Trochaic)

Christ is preached in Caesarea,
Caesar's city-next-the-sea;
Step by step the gospel reaches—
God of mercy!—you and me.

Peter hastens here from Joppa,
Saying nothing is unclean,
Saying God the Holy Spirit
Tells us what our visions mean.

Christ accepts a Roman soldier,
Worthy man, but not a Jew.
Did he not advise new wine-skins
When the wine of life is new?

Philip, on the road to Gaza,
As by chance, but Spirit-led,
Meets an Ethiopian stranger
Hungry for the living Bread.

There's a galley in the harbour
Taking Brother Paul to Rome:
By imprisonment and shipwreck,
Father, let your Kingdom come!

Christ was preached in Caesarea
By his faithful two or three:
This is how the gospel reaches
Others now: through you and me.

146 The Contemporary City

Pray for our cities! Grown too fast,
How many lives they crush or break!
Their golden nets too widely cast,
They gather more than they can take.
How many seeking gold find dross!
Who can assess the gain and loss?

Look kindly on each nameless face,
All who make up the motley throng:
That immigrant of alien race;
The lonely old, the rootless young;
The ones who rise, the ones who fall;
The rich, the poor: pray for them all!

What sins the great apostle saw
In Corinth, Athens, Ephesus!
What breaking of the moral law!
How these same problems stare at us,
From sordid sex to double-talk.
In modern London* or New York.

But Christ, who teaches us to care,
Who loved the city David planned,
Who wept for it, and suffered there;
Who builds on rock and not on sand:
He shares with us each urban task,
And gives new life to all who ask.

* "In San Francisco" was the original for use in America.

© For permission to reproduce this text, see page 239.

Other Ballads

147 God's Promise to Abraham C.M.
Genesis, 22, 1–19

When Father Abraham went out,
Not knowing where he went,
He trusted God to keep his word,
And therein was content.

How wonderful the promise was!
Said God: Look up and see:
As many as the stars of heaven
Shall your descendants be.

Said Abraham: I have no son!
Look down, said God, and see:
As many as these grains of sand
Shall your descendants be.

What joy when Sarah had a son!
What grief it was to slay
The little lad at God's command,
How bitter to obey!

But as he raised the ruthless knife,
Said God to Abraham:
Because you trusted me in this,
Behold, here is a lamb!

Now God fulfils his hidden plan:
A child of Jesse's stem,
The Lamb who died for all of us,
Is born in Bethlehem.

This hymn/carol was written in July, 1979, following correspondence about hymnody in general with the Rev. Dirk van Dissel (see **24**), by now Rector of Keith, South Australia, for use in the Christmas Service of Lessons and Carols at St. Catherine's Church, to the tune ST NICHOLAS (a melody from the eighteenth-century *The Spiritual Man's Companion*, as adapted in *Scottish Psalmody 1854*) or ST HUGH.

148 The Unlikely One

Now David was a shepherd boy
And Jesse's youngest son;
So skilful was he with sling and stone,
The wolves and jackals were scared of him,
And watched till he was gone.

Now David was too young for war,
And had to stay at home;
So skilful was he with the stringéd harp
The lambs and the grazing sheep looked up
When he began to strum.

Upon a day, to Jesse's door
There came a Man of God;
With snowy beard and a masterful eye,
He demanded to see all Jesse's sons—
For what, none understood.

Eliab and Abinadab,
Shammah and other four:
How handsome they were and strong of limb:
But each of them earned a shake of the head—
There must be one son more!

Come, little shepherd, leave your sheep,
And don't forget your sling;
You'll need your sling, and you'll need your harp,
And you'll slay Goliath, nine feet tall,
And God will make you King!

One meaning of this song is plain
To all who want to know;
When God himself has a job to be done,
It's you he may need, the unlikely one,
Though no one else thinks so!

This 1981 text was written in response to a letter from The Choristers' Guild, mentioning the need for biblical texts for Youth and Children's choirs.

149 In Honour of St. Andrew   8 8.6 6.

When Jesus walked by Galilee,
And cried to Andrew 'Follow me!'
He dropped his nets and went.
Would I were such a saint!

Though some were favoured more than he,
And he was fourth, and they 'the three',
Yet Andrew was content.
Would I were such a saint!

Of him they said, both Jew and Greek:
'Ask Andrew, if it's Christ you seek'.
He knew why they were sent.
Would I were such a saint!

So, far and wide, the legends prove
Here Andrew lived and here his love
Had taught men to repent.
Would I were such a saint!

Saint Andrew, wear a martyr's crown!
You were, in life and death, his own;
For him your life was spent.
Would I were such a saint!

This hymn was written in 1968 for a book Erik Routley hoped to produce. He composed a tune for it, STAWARD PEEL, named after a ruined fortified house overlooking the River Allen, a fine Northumbrian beauty-spot. (Erik was than a Minister of the Congregational Church serving in Newcastle.) The hymn was published in the Methodist Supplement *Hymns and Songs*. It had a 'preview' in worship at St. Andrew's Methodist Church, Worcester on the Sunday next St. Andrew's Day in 1968, and was sung in an illustrated lecture in Westminster Abbey in June 1969.

If there are personal likes and dislikes about words of hymns, this is yet more true of their tunes. In 1972, the Reverend R. R. Marshall, Minister of St. Magnus Presbyterian Church of Southern Africa at Randfontein in the Transvaal wrote to the editor of the *Expository Times* to seek help in finding another tune. Fred received this request and passed it on to Francis Westbrook, who composed HARPENDEN, which requires repetition of the last line of each verse. It was with Francis Westbrook's tune that the hymn appeared in 1974 in *Praise for Today*, the Baptist Supplement and in the Hymn Society of Great Britain and Ireland's Act of Praise booklet in 1975. It was sung at the memorial service for Francis in November 1975.

But South Africa still hankers after a Scottish melody for a hymn in honour of St. Andrew. In the meantime, a letter in Fred's sixth scrapbook from Hyla S. Watters, whose brother was sometime President of the Hymn Society of America, revealed its inclusion in a Festival of Hymns in the Galloway Methodist Church of Jackson, Mississippi in July 1973.

150 Magi or Kings?

7.6.7.6.

It may be they were Magi,
It may be they were kings,
Alighting from their camels
With smiles and offerings.

They gazed upon the infant
Who would be Lord of all,
And greatly were astounded
To find him in a stall.

Then rockéd they his cradle,
And offered gifts most rare;
And each gift had more meaning
Than any words can bear.

171

'We have but bread and wine, sirs;
It is but simple fare—
But what is ours', said Joseph,
'Is given us to share.'

Then Mary spread a white cloth
That she herself had spun,
And called them to the table
To celebrate her Son.

And when the meal was over,
Most joyful they had come,
They mounted on their camels
And headed them for home.

Now, in a distant country
They think upon these things:
More wise, if they are Magi,
More merciful, if kings.

This carol was written for a tune by United Reformed Church musician and lecturer Peter Cutts which he first conceived for Fred Kaan's hymn *The language of the Hebrews*. The tune MAGI has been re-named ST. OMEGALPH. It was first sung at Bandon Hill Methodist Church, Wallington, London on 21st December 1975, used by Fred as a personal Christmas card that year, and printed with the tune in the *Methodist Recorder*.

151 A Whistling Carol   C.M.

Who is it whistling on the hill
To keep himself awake?
Ben, the shepherd, it surely is,
Wishing the day would break.

Who is it whistling in the dark,
When all the flock is still?
Dan, the shepherd, it surely is,
Calling the dogs to heel.

Who is it whistling to his mates
And pointing to the sky?
Dave, the shepherd it surely is:
Glory to God on high!

Who is it whistling as they haste
To sleepy Bethlehem?
Three young shepherds, it surely is,
Come to adore the Lamb.

This carol was in response to a request from a Junior Choir Leader and was printed in the *Methodist Recorder* in 1973 with two whistling tunes, SHEPHERDS by David McCarthy and WHISTLING by Francis Westbrook. The text has been set as an anthem by the American composer, Hal Hopson, and also appeared in England in *Sing New Songs* (National Christian Education Council, 1981).

152 Shelter

All they wanted was a shelter,
Just a place to call their own,
But there wasn't room to house them
In that overcrowded town:
For it seems the Welfare Service
Was the sort that soon breaks down.
So don't sing alleluia
And don't sing gloria!

They were strangers. Galileans,
And the man a carpenter.
Though not quite the helpless people
Who are permanently poor,
No one beckoned them to enter
As they knocked from door to door.
So don't sing alleluia
And don't sing gloria!

She was pregnant, more's the pity,
And her time was not far off.
It's the awkward complication
That upsets a planner's graph:
If it wasn't so pathetic
It would make the angels laugh.
So don't sing alleluia
And don't sing gloria!

As we know, they found a lodging
In the backyard of an inn:
Not the best accommodation
She could have her baby in—
But it's all a God can hope for
When he's up against our sin.
So don't sing alleluia
And don't sing gloria!

But to know that his salvation
Is an all embracing care;
But to see what Christ is doing
And to find a way to share:
Is to sing our hymns and carols
As a challenge to despair.
Alleluia, alleluia
Alleluia, gloria!

In 1975, Fred was one of the judges in a competition organised by *Shelter*, the National Campaign for the Homeless in Great Britain. Besides judging the entries, he was moved to tackle this subject himself. This anti-hymn or anti-carol was the result. It was published in Shelter's booklet *Hymns for the Homeless* to a tune INSTEAD OF A CAROL by David McCarthy. It is equally effective, though, read without music.

153 The Donkey's Carol

7.7.7.7.5.
(Trochaic)

Here's a donkey you may trust;
While you can, escape you must!
When the baby had been fed:
Time to go, the donkey said.
Hey, Sir Donkey, hey!

Every day they lived in dread,
Little Saviour, make no sound:
Wicked men are prowling round!
Watch your step, the donkey said—
Hey, Sir Donkey, hey!

Out of Egypt, Israel fled;
Back to Egypt they must go.
Soft the sand, the going slow:
Take your time, the donkey said—
Hey, Sir Donkey, hey!

When the donkey disobeyed,
Joseph raised his stick in wrath.
There is danger in our path—
Think of Balaam, Mary said—
Hey, Sir Donkey, hey!

Where's the manna, magic bread?
Where's the water Moses struck,
For the thirsty, out of rock?
Trust in God, the donkey said—
Hey, Sir Donkey, hey!

175

Look, a city shines ahead!
Look at all the houses there!
Will they vanish into air?
Time will show, the donkey said—
Hey, Sir Donkey, hey!

Safe they are, with bed and board;
Safe and sound, our little Lord.
Till at last, King Herod dead:
Home we go, the donkey said:
Hey, Sir Donkey, hey!

The Latin Carol ORIENTIS PARTIBUS was originally a pilgrims' song
used on the route to Compostela and later was sung in France in the Middle
Ages on 14th January each year in processional celebration at the Festival of
the Donkey which commemorated the flight of the Holy Family into Egypt.
This prompted Fred to write this modern version for *The Galliard Book of
Carols* (1980). It was used in a dramatised telling of the story of the Holy
refugees during Family Worship at East Finchley Methodist Church,
London, on the Sunday nearest 14th January in 1981.

154 Tempted of Satan

Jesus Christ, for forty days
Tempted, for our sakes, to sin,
Face to face with Anti-Christ,
Won, as we must win.

'If you are what you presume,
Use these stones to feed the poor!'
Anti-Christ knows all the tricks,
Counts us one fool more.

176

'God will never let you down,
If you risk your neck for him!'
Anti-Christ can quote a text,
When it suits his theme.

'Conquer, then unite the world:
What a world it then could be!'
Anti-Christ will show us how,
If we bow the knee.

'By my Spirit', says the Lord;
'There can be no other way!'
Anti-Christ, defeated, goes;
Comes another day.

Jesus, in these testing times
Teach your servants how to know
Truth from error, right from wrong,
Friend from cunning Foe.

This hymn was first published in the *Methodist Recorder* on 13th February
1975. The tune suggested is CAPETOWN.

155 Jesus and the Storm

It was fair weather when we set sail,
The wind gentle, sunlight on our oars,
The lake peaceful as a sleeping child.
Who would have thought it could turn out so wild?

Jesus slept in the stern of the boat
As the sky darkened and the wind rose,
With huge waves, to a ten force gale.
First we lost the rudder and then the sail!

How tired the Master was to sleep so!
We woke him up, so great was our fright,
The terrible wind drowning our cry:
Do something! we cried, or we shall all die!

What he did then we shall never forget:
He rebuked us for our lack of faith,
Sternly commanding the storm to cease.
Who else could have spoken that word of peace?

This was written in 1980 in response to a general request from the Choristers'
Guild in Texas for material (anthem/song) suitable for children's and youth
choirs. Fred comments that in such writing strictness of metre is not as
necessary as in a hymn.

156 A Carol for Mothering Sunday

Mary sang to her Son: 'Don't you cry, little one!
Stars are peeping out at you and me,
And a thin crescent moon will be climbing soon
From the boughs of the judas tree!'

Mary saw how he grew out of shirt and of shoe,
How in stature he grew, and grace;
And was pleased that he played at the carpenters' trade,
As if born to take Joseph's place.

But her sorrows began after Jesus, as Man,
Had to do what he knew was right;
And her fears turned to woes when he faced his foes
On that harsh betrayal night.

Did she think of her joy in the babe and the boy,
When for us, as God's Son, he died,
And she stumbled uphill, with broken will,
The Mother of the Crucified.

We are glad, Lord, you came to an earthly home,
To depend on a woman's care;
Very precious to God must be motherhood,
For where love is found, God is there.

This carol was Fred's answer to a tune with an unusual rhythm sent to him by
Valerie Ruddle, and was printed in the *Methodist Recorder* in March, 1979.
The tune's title is MOTHERHOOD.

157 Song of Peter

We weren't dressed up in our Sabbath best
In our shawls of piety:
It might have been any fishing day
By the Lake of Galilee:
He didn't come to call righteous men,
He came to call you and me.

He called us three, and he called the Twelve,
To be of his company;
We quarrelled which of us should be chief,
Whether James or John or me:
He didn't come to call righteous men,
He came to call you and me.

The things he said and the things he did,
Are written in history,
But never all that he meant to us,
To James and John and me:
He didn't come to call righteous men,
He came to call you and me.

I swore I would go to prison or death
To prove my loyalty;
But I ran so fast I was out of breath,
When they nailed him to the Tree:
He didn't come to call righteous men,
He came to call you and me.

So now I say to Jew and Greek,
To bondmen and to free:
He is the one who can make us all
The men we ought to be:
He didn't come to call righteous men,
He came to call you and me.

This was written for a guitar group when Fred was Minister of Trinity
Methodist Church, Sutton, Surrey in 1965. The group knocked up a tune for
the one-off occasion—but later David McCarthy, Director of Music at
Woodhouse Grove, a Methodist public school in Yorkshire, set it as SONG
OF PETER to which music it was published in *26 Hymns* in 1971.

158 A Song of the Kingdom
Irregular

When Jesus came preaching the Kingdom of God
With the love that has power to persuade,
The sick were made whole, both in body and soul,
And even the demons obeyed.
But he needed a few he could trust to be true,
To share in his work from the start:
When Jesus came preaching the Kingdom of God,
God's gift to the humble of heart.

Since Jesus came preaching the Kingdom of God,
What a change in our lives he has made!
How many have shared in the joy of their Lord,
In self-giving have loved and obeyed!
But let none of us doubt what religion's about,
Or by what it is shamed and betrayed:
Do justly, love mercy, walk humbly with God,
Is the rule of life Jesus obeyed.

Still Jesus comes preaching the Kingdom of God
In a world that is sick and afraid;
His gospel has spread like the leaven in bread
By the love that has a power to persuade.
So let none of us swerve from our mission to serve,
That has made us his Church from the start,
May Jesus, the Light of the World, send us out
In the strength of the humble of heart.

In 1969, Francis Westbrook sent an arrangement of an old English melody. Fred wrote two texts, one entitled *A Song of the Humble of Heart* and the other *Christian Song for a Secular Festival*. Neither fitted the tune too well and he invited David McCarthy to try his hand at a tune to fit the words. But this did not really seem to work either, so Fred wrote a third version which was accepted for the Baptist Supplement *Praise for Today*. Another look was taken at both tunes: in the end Francis Westbrook made his tune fit the words more readily and this, entitled ACACIA, was used.

An anthem setting by Austin Lovelace is published by Triune Music, USA.

159 Nicodemus

7 7.7 7.
(Trochaic)

Nicodemus comes by night,
Seeking One who is the Light,
Fearful if he comes by day
He will give himself away.

Nicodemus must find out
What salvation is about;
He the worthiest of men,
Must, like us, be born again.

Scarcely he believes his ears:
Rabbi, he, these many years!
That he does not turn aside
Proves he overcomes his pride.

On a day when cowards run
He declares what side he's on;
Strangest of all gifts, he gives
Space in death—to One who lives.

This text written in 1978 responded to a commission from Lee Hastings
Bristol, Jnr. for ballads about New Testament characters and was set by him
for use in a Radio Series in the United States. It was also chosen as one of a
group of songs in *Partners in Praise* about incidents in the life of Jesus. Here
it was set to a new tune by Allen Percival: STRANGE SALVATION.

160 On the Jericho Road

A man had been robbed of all he had
On the Jericho Road;
They beat him up and left him for dead
'It happens like that,' the Master said,
'On the Jericho Road.'

A Priest and a Levite passed him by
On the Jericho Road;
They taught the Law but they didn't try
To help the man who was left to die
On the Jericho Road.

By chance a Samaritan passed that way
On the Jericho Road;
In spite of the worst the Jews could say,
He did his best for the man who lay
On the Jericho Road.

He bandaged him up with loving skill
On the Jericho Road,
And found an inn to care for him till
He came again (and settled the bill)
On the Jericho Road.

'To be a neighbour,' the Master said,
'On the Jericho Road,
Is to show compassion as that man did.'
For even faith without deeds is dead
On the Jericho Road,
On the Jericho Road,
On the Jericho Road.

Fred wrote this text with the guitar in mind and sent it in 1971 to the Secretary of 'Youth Makes Music', a course organised annually by the Methodist Church Music Society and the Methodist Association of Youth Clubs, hoping that some member of the course would compose a tune. David McCarthy (see **157**), Director of the Course that year, took it home himself. His tune NEIGHBOUR came effortlessly and he took the piece with him to a concert rehearsal he had previously arranged with Rita Morris. She was so delighted with the song that she sang it in Max Jaffa's show a few days later, on television. (David, who did not know Fred at the time, had to make several telephone calls to track him down for permission to use the song.) Since then, Rita Morris has frequently included it in recitals, recordings and in her BBC TV series 'She Shall Make Music'.

It is published in *26 Hymns*, the Baptist Supplement *Praise for Today*, and the ecumenical collection *Partners in Praise*.

161 The Lost Son

7.6.7.6.D.

All of you share my gladness:
The son I lost is found!
At last he's done with madness,
And back on solid ground.
Some have to learn the hard way
To tell the wheat from chaff:
Let there be songs and dancing,
And kill the fatted calf!

Great was my joy to see you,
As you came up the road!
What could I do but free you
From your unhappy load?
'Father, I'll be your servant'—
What could I do but laugh?
Let there be songs and dancing,
Dear son, on your behalf!

We must forgive your brother:
He's done the work of two,
But never tried to smother
His envy, son, of you.
Why should he be the loser,
Because the lost is found?
Let there be songs and dancing,
And pass the love-cup round!

After these years of sadness,
Of sorry news, or none,
Of wondering why such badness
Should come out in a son:
Let there be songs and dancing,
And pass the love-cup round!
Could God himself be happier?
The son I lost is found!

184

When working early in 1972 on the translation of a text set to Rudolf Zöbeley's lively, but rather tricky German tune ER WECKT MICH ALLE MORGEN, Fred dashed off some words to fix the metre in his mind. This unintended by-product of another piece of work found its way into the *Methodist Recorder* of March 1972. Later, Alan Dale wrote of it:

> ...it is singable as ballads should be, and it's fun—the kind of fun Jesus had which deepens genuine seriousness of purpose. Do write more....

The words were included in *Praise for Today* issued in 1974, set—to Fred's delight—to the original German tune which had inspired it. The text was revised somewhat in 1981.

162 The Tale of the Unjust Judge

It was Jesus who said we must persevere,
And told a tale to prove it:
The tale of a widow whose cause was good,
And a judge who wouldn't hear it.

Why the judge was unjust is not made clear,
I think my guess is a good one:
The widow had nothing to bribe him with,
And the bribe had to be a big one.

Did the widow give up? Good gracious, no!
Good gracious, not for a minute!
She showed her long face every judgement day,
And made sure the judge had seen it.

Oh it got on his nerves that long face of hers,
Her whining voice and her pleading.
'Get rid of her quickly' he told his clerk,
'You must give her what she's needing!'

So the judge gave way and the widow won,
Which shows it's worth persevering.
'That's how', said the Master, 'we have to pray,
Though our God is just and loving'.

This ballad was written in response to a request for texts based on Biblical incidents which were suitable for children. It was submitted as an entry in a competition jointly sponsored by the Hymn Society of America and The Choristers' Guild of America, but the entry was withdrawn when Fred was asked to be one of the judges! Valerie Ruddle (see **21**), who has taught music both in Great Britain and the Caribbean, provided a tune: PERSEVERANCE.

163 Be Ready

A Gospel Song for a Guitar Group

'You must be ready,' the Master said,
'Ready for what, Lord, ready for what?'
'Ready to wake up from the dead!'

'You must be ready,' the Master said,
'Ready for what, Lord, ready for what?'
'Ready to follow where I tread!'

'You must be ready,' the Master said,
'Ready for what, Lord, ready for what?'
'Ready to share my broken bread!'

'You must be ready,' the Master said,
'Ready for what, Lord, ready for what?'
'Ready to carry your cross, he said!'

'I am ready, Lord, ready,' I said,
'Ready to wake up from the dead,
Ready to follow where you tread,
Ready to share your broken bread,
Ready to carry my cross,' I said.
                    THEN I FLED!

A voice speaks as the guitar plays on:
'Do you really love me, Peter?'
and a voice replies:
'You know that I love you!'

'You must be ready,' the Master said,
'Ready for what Lord, ready for what?'
'Ready to feed my lambs,' he said.

This was first sung to the tune READY by David McCarthy at a *Youth Makes Music* Conference in Yorkshire in 1971. It was chosen for the Baptist Supplement *Praise for Today* in 1974. The second, third, fourth and final verses could be used as a hymn were a tune to be written in 9.9.8.

164 A Carol for Palm Sunday

'There's no room in the ark for donkeys,' said Shem;
'But the Good Lord,' said Noah, 'he created them.'

'It's their braying,' said Ham, 'gets under my skin;'
'But the Good Lord,' said Noah, 'puts up with the din.'

'They're as stubborn,' said Japheth, 'as original sin;'
'But the Good Lord,' said Noah, 'will break them in.'

'On a donkey,' they said, 'no proud man would ride;'
'But the Good Lord,' said Noah, 'hasn't got any pride—

On a donkey he'll ride, who must die for us all;
For the humblest may serve him, and they ever shall.'

The original version of this carol allowed for a refrain between each line:

'There's no room in the ark for donkeys,' said Shem;
All bells in Paradise I heard them ring.
'But the Good Lord,' said Noah, 'he created them.'
And I love sweet Jesus above anything.

It was written for John Wilson to the tune known as CORPUS CHRISTI CAROL, and was sung at Guildford Methodist Church on 26th March 1972. In its simplified version as above it awaits a tune.

165 A Carol for Easter Eve

8 6.8 6.8 8.
and Chorus

Good neighbours, do not ask them why
They hide their heads in shame,
For they have let their Master die,
And dare not name his Name.
It was but yesterday he died:
And who knows yet what shall betide?
He who died comes to reign!
Jesus shall reign!
On the Third Day rise again!

His sad disciples feel their loss
Weigh on them like a stone;
The soldiers, taking down the cross,
Count one more duty done.
It was but yesterday he died:
And who knows yet what shall betide?
Chorus

Today the promise falls apart;
The Kingdom does not come.
The Master died of broken heart;
And God himself is dumb.
It was but yesterday he died:
And who knows yet what shall betide?
Chorus

On such a day, the Day Between,
When all your hopes have fled,
O put your trust in things unseen,
In love that is not dead.
Lift up your hearts, all you who grieve:
Be not despairing, but believe!
Chorus

This carol, especially for Easter Eve, provides words of comfort for all in despair. It was commissioned by Bernard Braley as part of a set of new carol texts to old carol tunes, in this instance the sixteenth-century French UNE JEUNE PUCELLE. It appears in *The Galliard Book of Carols*.

166 Easter Day Carol

8.8.8.10.
and Chorus

What tale is this our women bring?
Who can believe so strange a thing?
An empty tomb? How can this be?
Where he was laid, there surely he must be!
Hurry, hurry, brothers; do not more delay:
Maybe it is true what the women say!

In this half-light, and half awake,
What simple errors one may make;
And fond illusions give relief
To hearts that bear so great a weight of grief.
Chorus

Pay we no heed to what he said,
Of how he talked of being dead,
And of those three mysterious days?
And did he not himself have power to raise?
Chorus

Let Brother Peter, Brother John,
Whose word we can rely upon,
Seek out the truth, so we may know
Where Jesus, whom we loved, and love, is now.
Chorus

They run, these two, and what they see
Shall be both truth and mystery:
For he, the Crucified, is risen,
No power on earth can silence or imprison.
Chorus

The tune is an old carol BURGUNDIAN NÖEL with the text *Promptement levez-vous ma voisin*, to which Fred set the Easter Story for *The Galliard Book of Carols*. He suggests that the first two verses might be sung as Male Solo, the second two verses as Female Solo, with the last verse and all choruses sung by everybody.

167 A Concert-goers' Carol

Turo, luro, luro, who can measure
All that music can impart?
Music gives unbounded pleasure
To the listening mind and heart.
In music's range
The smallest change
In pace or key
Can suddenly
Enchant us, enchant us.
These are moments of delight all the great composers grant us:
Giocoso,
Or maestoso,
All good music is the Lord's,
And offers us
Its rich rewards.

Turo, luro, luro, what a rondo!
What a strange, exciting beat!
How its final grand crescendo
Gets us tapping with our feet!
Relaxed, at ease,
And quiet, please,
Good people all,
Who fill this hall,
Discover, discover
No one has to read the score to become a music-lover.
None shall name us
Ignoramus
If our pleasure is sincere,
And makes us want
To stand and cheer.

Turo, luro, luro, brave conductor,
Tackling something new and hard;
He must know it tastes like nectar
Only to the avant-garde.
If what you hear
Insults the ear,
Forget the noise
And hear the voice
Of reason, of reason:
What displeases you tonight, you may learn to love next season!
Some disasters
Turn out masters.
All good music is the Lord's;
But who can say
What he applauds?

This humorous ballad reminds us all good music is the Lord's, punctures our
pomposity and laughs at our prejudice. Does it belong with the other writing
in the book? No? Yes? But didn't our Lord so often tell the truth with a
twinkle in his eyes? It was written for *The Galliard Book of Carols* to a
Traditional Basque Melody here named TURO LURO LURO. Fred noted
this as the sober version: his first draft was much more cheeky.

191

168 A Herb Carol

When God created herbs
He gave them work to do:
Sweet Marjoram has flavour,
Bergamot has fragrance,
Rosemary cures headaches
(And these are but a few);
Then Satan planted Rue.
When God created herbs,
Then Satan planted Rue,
The sad, mysterious Rue.

So Eve made use of herbs
That in her garden grew:
Sweet Marjoram for flavour,
Bergamot for fragrance,
Rosemary for headaches
(And these were but a few);
But she was piercèd through.
So Eve made use of herbs,
But she was piercèd through
When Adam plucked the Rue.

Our Lady loved the herbs
That in her garden grew:
Sweet Marjoram for flavour,
Bergamot for fragrance,
Rosemary for headaches
(And these were but a few);
But she was piercèd through.
Our Lady loved the herbs,
But she was piercèd through
When Jesus plucked the Rue.

All you who dote on herbs
And praise the good they do;
Sweet Marjoram for flavour,
Bergamot for fragrance,
Rosemary for headaches
(And these are but a few);
Lest you be piercèd through,
All you who dote on herbs,
Lest you be piercèd through,
Let none you love touch Rue.

Fred accepted a commission to write contemporary texts on many subjects for *The Galliard Book of Carols.* As a note to this one he added:

> The common rue (*Ruta graveolens*) has long had a double reputation. The plant was much used in medieval times as a stimulative and irritant drug. It was commonly supposed to be used by witches. From its association with 'rue' (sorrow, repentance), the plant was also known as the 'herb of grace'. For the purpose of this medieval-style carol I have made rue a bad thing!

The music THE RUE is a transcription of John Dowland's lutesong *Now cease my wandering eyes* (1600), incorporating the tune.

169 A Mistletoe Carol

Say you this pagan mistletoe
Is fit to bring us nought but woe?
Rejoice that he who came that night redeems us all:
Deck the branches! Light the candles! Sing Nowell, Nowell!

Say you these holly berries red
Are drenched in sacrificial blood?
Chorus

Say you this Christian holy day
Was first a pagan holiday?
Chorus

Say you our Christian joy recalls
Wild Saturnalian carnivals?
Chorus

Rejoice that he who came that night
Turns pagan darkness into light!
Chorus.

This carol builds on the way our Christian celebrations mix old pagan customs with the Christian story. It was written for *The Galliard Book of Carols* to a traditional Dutch tune of the fifteenth century which a Frenchman had earlier used for a carol about mistletoe (*Le frêle gui*). It has also been published in a new selection for choirs, *32 Galliard Carols for Christmas* with its tune, MISTLETOE.

170 Shrove Tuesday Carol

So toss, toss, toss the golden pancake,
Wash it down with ale:
The only thing that we can take
To heaven's a ransomed soul!

Friends, we begin tomorrow
The forty days of Lent:
Today we'll banish sorrow,
And feast to our content:
Chorus

194

Tomorrow we shall mourn them,
Our pleasure-loving ways,
Give up our sins or pawn them,
And fill our mouths with praise:
Chorus

Tomorrow, meekly shriven,
We'll turn our backs on hell,
Resume our path to heaven,
And know that all is well:
Chorus (*repeat last line*)

This was one request to Fred for *The Galliard Book of Carols.* In a note about the carol Fred wrote:

In medieval times the day before Ash Wednesday (the first day of Lent) came to be known as Shrove Tuesday or Pancake Day. On this day Christians were 'shriven' (confessed their sins and received absolution) in preparation for Lent; but it was also a day of feasting before enforced abstinence, hence the pancakes. The popular attitude to the day is recaptured in this modern carol.

The tune is also called SHROVE TUESDAY CAROL.

195

IV

TRANSLATIONS

Fred wishes it to be made clear that he is no linguist and that consequently he has to rely on a literal translation by someone who is. His task is to versify not translate. The real difficulty is to make the verse fit the tune to which the original hymn is sung, especially if the language belongs to a different group, say Spanish or Welsh.

Cantate Domino

The first hymns in this section were written in the three years before the publication in 1974 of *Cantate Domino*, a new edition of the international hymn-book published for the World Council of Churches. Erik Routley turned to Fred for a number of translations, many with unusual rhythms.

171 Blest be the King

14.13.13 13.

Blest be the King whose coming is in the name of God!
For him let doors be opened, no hearts against him barred!
Not robed in royal splendour, in power and pomp comes he:
But clad as are the poorest—such his humility.

Blest be the King whose coming is in the name of God!
By those who truly listen his voice is truly heard.
Pity the proud and haughty, who have not learned to heed
The Christ who is the Promise and has our ransom paid.

Blest be the King whose coming is in the name of God!
He only to the humble reveals the face of God.
All power is his, all glory! All things are in his hand,
All ages and all peoples, till time itself shall end!

Blest be the King whose coming is in the name of God!
He offers to the burdened the rest and grace they need.
Gentle is he and humble! And light his yoke shall be,
For he would have us bear it so he can make us free.

From the Spanish of the Uruguayan writer, Frederico J. Pagura, set to a
melody by Homere Perera.

172 Deliver us, Lord Jesus

Come to us who wait here; and tarry not!
You only can deliver us, Lord Jesus.

Out of our world, out of its distress,
We call on you, Lord Jesus.
Chorus

A love much stronger than our sadness
Has made us one, Lord Jesus.
Chorus

In all our anguish, all our darkness,
We search for you, Lord Jesus.
Chorus

And in our discords, though they wound you,
We plead with you, Lord Jesus.
Chorus

You came among us once, a poor man,
To save us all, Lord Jesus.
Chorus

And in our night, your Cross of Sorrow
Shall be our hope, Lord Jesus.
Chorus

But when, at last, your day is dawning
We shall see you, Lord Jesus.
Chorus

Translated from the French of Dominique Ombrie, who provided the music.

173 The Feast of Christmas   5.6.5.6.7.5 7.

All the sky is bright,
Filled with joy, a new joy.
Waiting for the night
We will talk of wonders.
Never was a Feast like this!
Born is Jesus Christ,
Born the Child-God given to us!

Now our Lord appears,
He whose word enlightens;
All creation hears
Of the Father's goodness.
He, the God of this poor earth,
He has come to show
Where our wandering steps should go.

Not alone they come,
Simple shepherds, wise men:
All the human race
Wants to make him welcome,
Wants to look upon the face
Of the Lord of bliss,
Who becomes a child for us.

Glory be to Christ,
Glory to the Father's Son,
And the Holy Ghost,
He whose love enlightens!
Dazzling is the mystery
Filling all the sky:
To the Man-God *Glory!* cry.

From the French of Claude Rozier, to a traditional Auvergne melody.

174 The Word is Born

Lo! Today into our world the Word is born,
To declare to man the Father's deep love and concern.
Heaven itself teaches us how great the mystery:
Glory to God and peace on earth, alleluia!

Lo! Today into our darkness has shone the Light,
To restore eyesight to men who are groping in night.
All his vast universe bathes in his mystery:
Glory to God and peace on earth, alleluia!

Lo! Today into our death the Life breaks in,
To transform the hearts of men who are hardened by sin.
Love shall be stronger far than all our misery:
Glory to God and peace on earth, alleluia!

Lo! Today into our flesh the Lord descends,
To unite the men who wait to be counted his friends.
Off'ring him to his Father, Mary kneels rev'rently:
Glory to God and peace on earth, alleluia!

From the French of Didier Rimaud, to an adaptation of the plainchant
JESU REDEMPTOR.

175 A New Song

Sing to the Lord a new song, for he does wonders.
God triumphs, for he is righteous,
And his sacredness is his strength;
The Lord has declared his saving power,
He everywhere displays his righteousness.

Chorus
You think God is the Unknown One,
That his power is of small account?
That God can't see what oppresses you?
Look at your life, how he takes care of it.

Often you don't know his purpose
Or what is the right thing to do;
But God sends his help to everyone
Who truly seeks to understand his will.

Chorus
You must learn to see him only
As the Father who guides your life;
This very day he holds out his hand;
So seize it now and do not turn away.

From the German of Paulus Stein, to music by Rolf Schweizer.

176 Images of the Cross

By the Cross which did to death our only Saviour,
This blessed vine from which grapes are gathered in:
Jesus Christ, we thank and bless you!
By the Cross, which casts down fire upon our planet,
This burning bush in which love is plainly shown:
Jesus Christ, we glorify you!
By the Cross on Calvary's hill securely planted,
This living branch which can heal our every sin:
Conquering God, we your people proclaim you!

By the Blood with which we marked the wooden lintels
For our protection the night when God passed by:
Jesus Christ, we thank and bless you!
By the Blood, which in our Exodus once saved us,
When hell was sealed up by God's engulfing sea:
Jesus Christ, we glorify you!
By the Blood which kills the poison in bad fruitage,
And gives new life to the dead sap in the tree:
Conquering God, we your people proclaim you!

By the Death on Calvary's hill of him the First-born,
Who bears the wood and the flame of his own pyre:
Jesus Christ, we thank and bless you!
By the Death, amid the thorns, of God's own Shepherd,
The Paschal Lamb who was pierced by our despair:
Jesus Christ, we glorify you!
By the Death of God's Beloved outside his vineyard,
That he might change us from murderer into heir:
Conquering God, we your people proclaim you!

By the Wood which sings a song of nuptual gladness,
Of God who takes for his Bride our human race:
Jesus Christ, we thank and bless you!
By the Wood which raises up in his full vigour
The Son of Man who draws all men by his grace:
Jesus Christ, we glorify you!
By the Wood where he perfects his royal priesthood
In one High Priest who for sin is sacrifice:
Conquering God, we your people proclaim you!

Holy Tree which reaches up from earth to heaven
That all the world may exult in Jacob's God:
Jesus Christ, we thank and bless you!
Mighty Ship which snatches us from God's deep anger,
Saves us, with Noah, from drowning in the Flood:
Jesus Christ, we glorify you!
Tender Wood which gives to brackish water sweetness,
And from the Rock shall strike fountains for our good:
Conquering God, we your people proclaim you!

From the French of Didier Rimaud, to music by Josef Gelineau (see also
184).

177 Yours be the Glory

Yours be the glory, yours, O Risen Friend!
You have won the victory that shall never end!
O how bright an angel rolls the stone away:
Conquered is the tomb in which your body lay!
Yours be the glory, yours, O Risen Friend!
You have won the victory that shall never end!

See, here is Jesus! who else could it be?
He, your Lord and Saviour, surely it is he!
Happy Church of Jesus, you who doubt no more,
Never cease to tell us Christ is conqueror!
Chorus

He lives forever! Bid me fear no more;
He is Prince of Peace, the one whom I adore.
With him to support me, victory shall be won:
Now, my life, my glory, every fear is gone!
Chorus

A new translation following more nearly the French original of Edmund Budry.

178 Seeking Wisdom

We would ask, Lord, for your Spirit!
It is he who gives us your strength:
So we newly understand the old
And find that God is near us
We would ask, Lord, for your Spirit!

We would ask, Lord, for your Spirit!
It is he who gives us your strength:
We don't want just to ask the questions:
We want to know the answer.
We would ask, Lord, for your Spirit.

We would ask, Lord, for your Spirit.
It is he who gives us your strength.
Though we are frightened we might lose heart,
We still may risk the answer.
We would ask, Lord, for your Spirit.

From the German of Dieter Trautwein, to a tune by H. R. Siemoneit.

179 Awake, Sleeping Church

Sun of Righteousness, arise,
Now today, in our own skies;
In your Church's dawning be
That one light by which men see.
Have mercy, Lord.

Wake dead Christianity,
Sleeping in complacency;
May it listen to you, Lord,
Turn again and trust your Word.
Have mercy, Lord.

See your Church by troubles rent
Men were helpless to prevent;
Gather, Shepherd of us all,
Those who stumble, stray, and fall.
Have mercy, Lord.

205

Open wide your people's doors;
May no guile, no earthly powers,
Do your Kingdom harsh despite.
Lord, create in darkness light.
Have mercy, Lord.

Give your servants from above
Faith and courage, hope and love;
Let rich harvests there be grown
Where they have in sorrow sown.
Have mercy, Lord.

Let us see your glory now
As about the world we go;
With our little strength increase
Whatsoever makes for peace.
Have mercy, Lord.

Every honour, glory, praise,
Shall the Highest have always;
So that in the Three-in-one
We ourselves shall be at one.
Have mercy, Lord.

From the German of Christian David, Christian Gottlob Barth, and
Christian Nehring, compiled by Otto Riethmuller. Erik Routley's letter
sending this for translation records:

> *Sonne der Gerechtigkeit* is something of a curiosity. As you will
> see, its present form is written by no fewer than four authors,
> three of whom are called 'Christian'! It is one of the very few old
> German hymns—indeed the only one of the eighteenth century
> —that the Germans have asked for in *Cantate Domino*: and
> looking over some modern and trendy German hymn-books I
> find that it is never omitted, whatever else is....

180 The Vital Word

8 8.7.8.

Your voice, my God, calls me by name;
Your joy awaits me in your home.
Dearest Lord, your kindly word
Fails me never, stands for ever.

Your death, my Jesus, sets me free;
Your life has risen again in me.
Dearest Lord, your vital word
Activates me, captivates me.

Spirit of Love, repeat that sign
Which makes anew this heart of mine.
Dearest Lord, now is your word
Shining o'er me, praying for me.

From the French of Claude Rozier, to a tune by Erik Routley, CARTIGNY.

181 Honoured Guest

Lord, you are at many tables
An invited, honoured Guest.
Even of those, Lord
Who are self-sufficient
You let none bear you down.
Come, share the meal with us,
Come, share the meal with us,
Unite those who part without loving.

Lord, you are at many tables
An invited, honoured Guest.
You also speak, Lord,
To those who see nothing
Except tomorrow's cares.
Come, share the meal with us,
Come, share the meal with us,
Give light to the eyes of the weary.

Lord, you are at many tables
An invited, honoured Guest.
You come to people
Who do without you.
False piety, you hate.
Come, share the meal with us,
Come, share the meal with us,
Then, Lord we shall trust what you offer.

Lord, you are at many tables
An invited, honoured Guest.
But as our Host, Lord,
You make sure we carry
Each other's load of cares.
Come, share the meal with us,
Come, share the meal with us,
Here, now, and at each of our tables.

From the German of Dieter Trautwein, to a tune by the author.

182 Members of the Body of Christ

Lord, let us listen when you speak!
Speak through the words that we are using!
Help us to obey you, Lord!
Lord, let us listen when you speak!
You are Christ's Feet here today in the world:
Go discover all the people who are most in need!

Chorus
You are Christ's Eyes here today in the world:
Look behind all our pretences when injustice shouts!

Chorus
You are Christ's Hands here today in the world:
So, by grasping life do all the good you can and should!

Chorus
You are Christ's Lips here today in the world:
Speak of that amazing rescue he has carried out!

From the German of Dieter Trautwein and Kurt Rummel, to a melody by
Dieter Trautwein.

183 Night Thoughts

7.6.7.6.D.

The night is nearly over
The daylight nearly here:
With praises let us welcome
God's bright and morning star.
Who suffered long in darkness
Join in the joyful strain:
The morning star is shining
On all your fear and pain.

He who was served by angels
Comes as a child to serve:
For God in mercy tempers
The justice we deserve.
Whoever here is guilty,
Who knows himself defiled:
Look up! and find salvation
Believing in this Child.

How quickly night is passing—
Haste to the stable now!
There you will find salvation,
The reason why and how.
God from your guilt's beginning
Has heard you when you cried.
Now he whom God has chosen
Is standing at your side.

As long as nights are falling
On human guilt and pain,
The star of God's good pleasure
Will shine on travelling men.
In souls lit by its radiance
The darkness cannot brood:
Look up! salvation for you
Shines from the face of God!

God wants to live in darkness
So he can make it bright;
As though he would reward it
He guides the world aright.
He who created all things
Does not forsake the lost;
Who trusts the Son as Saviour
Has freedom at the last.

From the German of Jochen Klepper (1903–1942), considered by many to be the most important twentieth-century hymn writer from Germany. A journalist who worked on Christian radio programmes, he published *Kyrie*, a book of hymns, in 1938. The tune used in *Cantate Domino* DIE NACHT IST VORGEDRUNGEN is by Johannes Petzold, a professor of Church Music in East Germany. Following the suggestion of John Wilson, the text above incorporates some small changes and is printed as it was sung at an Act of Praise in Manchester Cathedral on the occasion of a Hymn Society Conference in 1978.

184 New Year Greeting from Prison   11.10.11.10.

By gracious powers so wonderfully sheltered,
And confidently waiting come what may,
We know that God is with us night and morning
And never fails to greet us each new day.

Yet is this heart by its old foe tormented,
Still evil days bring burdens hard to bear.
O give our frightened souls the sure salvation
For which, O Lord, you taught us to prepare.

And when this cup you give is filled to brimming
With bitter suffering, hard to understand,
We take it thankfully and without trembling,
Out of so good, and so beloved, a hand.

Yet when again, in this same world, you give us
The joy we had, the brightness of your sun,
We shall remember all the days we lived through,
And our whole life shall then be yours alone.

Now, when your silence deeply spreads around us,
O let us hear all your creation says—
That world of sound which soundlessly invades us,
And all your children's highest hymns of praise.

The text, based on Dietrich Bonhoeffer's New Year Message to his Friends
smuggled out of prison, was set to music by Josef Gelineau, the French priest
well known for his psalm settings for choir and congregation. As a hymn it is
usually sung to INTERCESSOR, the last verse being omitted. In this form it
appears in several hymn-books.

Llyfr Carolau Deiniol

When the Bangor Diocesan Music Committee was planning *Llyfr Carolau Deiniol* (*St. Deiniol Carol Book*) published in 1974 the editor, Alan Luff (see **68**) sent Fred several old Welsh Carols. His request was for English words, catching perhaps the theme of the Welsh, but which captured the elaborate rhyme structure, including the internal rhyming, of the originals. This is in the spirit of a long tradition since many generations of Welsh poets have felt free to write words for these tunes.

185 How near he is, how dear

8.6.8.6.D.
(D.C.M.)

This carol we will gladly sing
To all with ears to hear,
So we may show you Jesus Christ,
How near he is, how dear!
Yes, yes, it was at Bethlehem
That Jesus Christ was born,
But Bethlehem is any town
And this is Christmas morn!

For any hill could be the hill
Where glory shone around,
And any shepherd out at night
Stumble on holy ground.
Though it was many miles from here
Where Jesus Christ was born,
How near he is, how dear he is,
And this is Christmas morn!

For any star could be the star,
And any inn the inn,
And any byre could be the byre
By loving hands swept clean.
Though it was many years ago
When Jesus Christ was born,
How near he is, how dear he is,
And this is Christmas morn!

This carol we will gladly sing
At any open door,
So we may show you Jesus Christ,
Who lives for evermore.
Because it was for each of us
That Jesus Christ was born,
How near he is, how dear he is,
And this is Christmas morn!

The words have no relation to the Welsh original. The charming original
tune DIFYRRWCH GWYR CAENARFON (*The delight of the men of
Caernarvon*) was first sung to the English text at Heartsease Lane Methodist
Church, Norwich, at Christmas 1973. It was sung to a new tune,
CHRISTMAS MORN, by Michael Dawney in *Christmas Music for the
Family* at Poole Arts Centre in December 1981.

213

186 Hosanna!

Hosanna! Come and see
One born for you and me:
Maker of all things on his Mother's knee!
Then keep this Festival
And thankfully recall
Christ lived and died and rose again for all.
Look how he stoops to such as I,
To raise us up and lift us high!
Look how he shares his glory
By laying glory by!
By dying he has sweetened death,
By rising fortified our faith.
By giving us his Spirit
Filled us with his own breath.

He who in manger lies,
Is he the one who dies
Whom each man in his own way crucifies?
What miracle is this,
That we should come to bliss
Through such a sacrificial love as his!
We need not wait one instant more
For Christ is knocking on the door;
So this day let us welcome
This Child whom we adore.
Now shall the heedless learn their need;
Now shall our captive souls be freed,
And each of us find selfhood
Through Christ's atoning deed.

Fred uses some of the ideas in the original Welsh text *Hosanna! Dyma'r Dydd*
(*Hosanna, this is the day*). The carol tune is DIFYRRWCH GWYR Y
GOGLEDD (*The delight of the men of the North*) and was sung in Bangor
Cathedral in December 1974.

214

187 Shepherds and Wise Men

As Jesus Christ lay fast asleep
And bedded in a manger,
Some simple shepherds left their sheep
To find the Heavenly Stranger.
The Morning Star that shone so bright
On travelling men benighted
Their footsteps guided to the place where,
                          kneeling they recited:
For joy of the Boy we will sing you this carol,
Though gruff are our voices and rough our apparel:
God make you right merry this Christmas!
Though sheep may be stupid, they know they must follow
The shepherd who leads them by hillside and hollow:
God make you right merry this Christmas!

As Wise Men guided by a star
Alighted at that manger,
They wondered why they came so far
To find so small a stranger;
But being wise they thought again,
And owned themselves delighted
That God was speaking through a child, so,
                          kneeling they recited:
Though wise men are foolish, they know they must follow
Wherever truth leads them by hillside or hollow:
So God make you merry this Christmas!
As sign that our sorrows say more than our pleasures,
For joy of the Boy we offer these treasures:
So God make you merry this Christmas!

In this translation Fred has kept more closely to the original Welsh. The
tune, dug out of the archives of Bangor University by Alan Luff, is called
FFARWEL NED PUW meaning *Farewell to Ned Pugh*, reputedly a
drunken fiddler who is said to have disappeared into a cave and whose
fiddling can still be heard coming from underground!

215

188 When he came

10 10. 7 7. 10 10.

Angelic hosts proclaimed him, when he came,
                    when he came,
Our Lord and Saviour named him, when he came.
As David's town lay dreaming
That night of our redeeming,
How few there were esteemed him, when he came,
                    when he came;
Poor peasant's child they deemed him, when he came.

His love for us has pleaded, his alone, his alone;
His sacrifice is needed, his alone.
He whose forgiveness freed us
Shall by his Spirit lead us
Whose flocks are safely feeding, his alone, his alone,
No other voices heeding, his alone.

All you who need protection, come to him, come to him,
Against the world's infection, come to him;
You who no hope expected,
Defeated and dejected:
You who have life rejected, come to him, come to him,
Himself the Resurrected, come to him.

His seed in secret growing, everywhere, everywhere,
Has now its winter sowing, everywhere.
What love it takes—how slowly!—
To make one sinner holy:
But Christ has for his showing, everywhere, everywhere,
Harvests beyond our knowing, everywhere.

A winner if ever I saw one—I can understand you sweating
over that rhyme scheme,.,,, Thanks and congratulations.

So Alan Luff thanked Fred for his English words. In sending Fred his brief
about John Davies' nineteen-verse hymn, Alan had written:

> This goes on for 19 verses!—the child in the temple, the betrayal
> (with chorus 'in the garden'): trial, crucifixion (with chorus 'on
> the cross'); and ends with some heavy moralizing with the chorus
> 'true enough'! Its last verse uses a common trick in these carols
> and, with great ingenuity but not much subtlety, manages to get
> the date in (it's rather like trying to work out Roman numerals).
> However I have given you the verses in which I think there are
> some quite good ideas, and some pleasant twists with the chorus,
> although they are not all in fact viable in Welsh because of some
> terrible lines.

The metre is called *Mentra Gwen* and the tune was found by Alan Luff
in Bangor University Archives. It is a particularly graceful form of
TWRGWYN by the nineteenth-century composer John Edwards of
Llangadog. John Wilson notes how refreshing it is to find a Welsh tune which
does not wallow in the everlasting AABA form. In 1978 Alan Luff drew
attention in *The Hymn* to the fact that this metre is, with changes that depend
on the nature of the Welsh language, that of WONDROUS LOVE.

The December 1978/January 1979 issue of *NOW*, the magazine of the
Overseas Division of the Methodist Church, centred on music round the
world. This text, omitting verse 3, with its Welsh tune, featured England and
Wales at one stroke.

189 A Vision of Angels   9.8.9.8.D.

How dark was the night of his coming!
How bleak was the wind on the hill!
How many who slept till cock-crowing
Had little to wake for but ill.
Good shepherds, who stare into heaven,
What see you so fair and so rare?
What glory transfigures your faces?
What songs are enchanting the air?

217

Those dutiful shepherds saw angels
Where most of us only see night;
Their beautiful vision escapes us
Who cease to believe in the light.
The song is tossed back into darkness
By winds that are bitter with hate;
But shepherds have found in a manger
That Saviour the ages await.

You angels, we see you, we hear you!
We stand with our backs to the wind!
The longer we listen, the stronger
Your message of hope for mankind.
You sceptics and cynics, forgive us
For leaving you out in the cold:
We'll come back with songs of salvation,
Good news that shall never grow old.

Besides inclusion in the *St. Deiniol Carol Book* this was used later with minor amendments in *Partners in Praise*. It was sung to YR HEN DDARBI (OLD DERBY) in Alan Luff's arrangement in Bangor Cathedral on 8th December 1974. An anthem setting by Austin Lovelace is issued by Augsburg Publishing House, USA.

Other Translations

190 The Indwelling Christ

8.7.8.7.
(Iambic)

O Jesus Christ; as you awake
In me, all else effacing,
My heart is daily nearer you,
And further off from sinning.

Your gracious favour, day by day,
Surrounds my every weakness;
Your light has overcome my night,
Your life embraced my dying.

Let all your wisdom, joy, and grace
Shine in and through my spirit,
That others in my bliss or grief
May see your living likeness.

The more I seek, with honest zeal,
To serve you in your kingdom,
The more I flee from trivial aims,
From all that feeds self-glory.

Lord, I believe yours is the power
That gives my life direction;
You are my great, my chief desire,
My joy, my inspiration.

Although rejected by the editors who asked for it, Fred retained the belief that this new translation of *O Jesus Christus, wachs' in mir* was worthwhile. His fellow member of the Norwich Writers' Circle, Melville Hastings, made a new literal translation of the ten verses of the German original by Johann Caspar Lavater. Elizabeth Lee Smith's famous and deeply mystical hymn, *O Jesus Christ, grow thou in me* used verses 1, 2, 3, 5, 6 and 8 and opted for common metre. Fred used verses 1, 2, 5, 7 and 10, retaining the German metre. This is a rare example in Fred's work of a hymn without rhyme. The German tune suggested is ACH GOTT UND HERR.

191 The Famous Fast

L.M.

Now, as we keep this famous fast,
Let us be taught its sacred use:
So when these forty days are past
The good we gain may not be lost.

What God in ancient law revealed,
And prophets by example sealed,
The Christ of every season, Lord,
Hallowed for us in deed and word.

Then let us use more sparingly
What we find hardest to forgo,
That, standing steadfast, we may be
Grounded in Christian liberty.

Thus may we shun all evil things
That make us Satan's underlings,
All that diverts us from the good
And justly earns the wrath of God.

Our sins, Lord, humbly we confess:
Though we are frail, we are your own.
Forgive the evil we have done,
And what is good in us increase.

Help us, most Blessed Trinity,
By your unchanging Unity,
To reap, before you call us hence
The harvest of our penitence.

This paraphrase of the sixth-century Latin Office Hymn *Ex more docti mystico* was written in 1974 at the request of Dirk van Dissel (see **24**). The recommended tune is EISENACH (*Hymns Ancient and Modern, revised*, 187).

192 Your Kingdom come on Earth...

What is our earth but a prison
Where millions, despairing, lie?
Women are selling their bodies:
In darkness our children die.
Next to the palace of marble
Shanty-town sweats in the heat;
Instead of loving there's violence,
Rancour and hate in our streets.
Soon may we see your will done on earth, Lord.
Soon may we see its coming, your Reign of love.

This, Jesus, isn't your Kingdom;
It cannot be, Lord, your will
Brothers should be disunited
While hunger and torture kill.
This is why, turning to heaven
In our confusion, we pray:
Lord, may your Kingdom come quickly;
Shine, sun, on our world today.
Chorus

When Jesus lived here among us
He said: 'I am this world's Light;
Soon as my truth shines within you
My freedom will be in sight:
In me there can be no barriers,
Sects and divisions must cease;
One in my truth and compassion,
You shall abide in my peace.'
Chorus

Fulfil your promise, Lord Jesus:
Let your Kingdom of Love appear;
Soon may the sun of your justice
Give light to your people here.
Cleanse us, your church, of corruption;
Lift us above our despair:
Then through your love and your presence,
Our earth shall be once more fair.
Chorus

A special edition of the World Council of Churches Quarterly *Risk* was published in 1975 to serve as a Worship Book for use of the Fifth Assembly of the World Council of Churches that year at Nairobi. Fellow hymn-writer Fred Kaan, one of the editors of the Worship Book, wrote on behalf of the WCC on 18th December 1974 seeking Fred's help in providing an English setting of a Spanish hymn by F. J. Pagura. Enclosed was the contemporary music by Pablo Sosa and a literal translation of the text. They suggested that four verses of English might replace the five of Spanish. Fred telescoped the first two Spanish verses of protest into one, helping 'to give full weight to Pagura's Christian answer'. In his scrapbook Fred refers to this task as a ferociously difficult assignment: nevertheless the deadline of 24th January 1975 was still in the far distance when, Christmas mails notwithstanding, the English text reached Geneva on 3rd January! The hymn was also translated into French by Etienne de Peyer.

193 Jesus our Redeemer

8 8.8 8.

Jesus, how strong is our desire
To love you, our Redeemer, more,
You who, in God's creative plan,
Became, in latter times, a man.

What mercy moved you, loving Lord,
To bear the sinner's bitter load,
And by your own death on the Tree
From death's dominion set us free?

You stormed the very gate of hell,
Released the captive from his cell,
In noblest triumph took your place
Upon your Father's throne of grace.

By that same mercy spare us still,
Grant us the power to conquer ill,
And in your presence find at last
The deep fulfilment which is rest.

And this shall be our true reward
To share the triumph of our Lord,
That in the Father, Spirit, Son,
All shall be one, as God is one.

This translation of the ancient Latin Ascensiontide hymn of the seventh or
eighth century was made following correspondence with Dirk van Dissel (see
24), who has a special interest in the hymns of early Christendom. This
particular Latin text began *Jesu nostra redemptio*. The free churches, to their
loss, have tended to ignore the rich heritage of these early Hymns for the
Office. A suggested tune is WINCHESTER NEW.

194 Grant us your Light

You, dear Lord, resplendent within our darkness,
                                    grant us your light.
This heart of mine is in deep anguish,
                    I feel so far off, so far from you.
How sad our life, Lord, if you should leave us,
                    if you should leave us without your light.

Chorus
This night I follow in your footsteps, but cannot
                            clearly behold your light.
You, Lord, must guide us throughout our lifetime,
                    throughout our lifetime to that clear light.

Chorus
We soon shall see the new day dawning, shall see
          the dawning of eternal light.
May we in loving and peaceful living behold
          together your endless light.

In August 1981 Fred met Dr Gerhard H. Cartford, of the South American state of Colombia, at the Oxford International Hymnody Conference. Dr Cartford, an American working in Colombia and a musician, asked Fred to co-operate with him in providing English translations of Spanish hymns in use in Colombian Christian churches. Supplied with a literal translation of the Spanish, and Dr Cartford's own tune, the partnership opened with this hymn, which has the Spanish title *Danos tu luz*.

195 A Vision of Heaven   9.8.9.8.D.

The fountain of joy is in Heaven:
What brightness, what glory is there!
For there has my Jesus ascended,
To make us for ever his care.
The Blood that was shed for us sinners
In purity pleads our release;
So rich it redeems us from prison,
Gives life to the dying—and peace.

To those for whom life is a desert,
How welcome must Paradise be!
The self-weary soul shall find rest there,
From life's agitations set free.
Secure from whatever assaults us,
Whatever has put us to shame,
We'll share there, with songs of rejoicing,
The ineffable love of the Lamb.

Look down from the towers of Zion:
Life's journey is spread at our feet!
The bitterest trials we suffered
Shall yield us rewards that are sweet.
Safe-harboured from tempest and shipwreck,
Delivered from death and the grave,
We'll pray to the Lord for the living,
Who only is able to save.

This 'vision' is based on the Welsh funeral hymn *Mae ffrydiau'ngorfoledd yn tarddu* by David Charles (1762–1834) and sung to the tune CRUGYBAR. In 1981 Fred's friend, retired schoolmaster E. G. Hutchings, called his attention to the tune, saying it was frequently sung at funerals in Wales. But to what text? Alan Luff, who is now widely acknowledged as an authority on Welsh hymnody, was able to let Fred have a literal translation. In his letter he observed:

> As far as I can see, the last verse ends by saying: 'When I get to heaven I shall sit back and watch all you suckers there below sweating it out'.

In a case like this the modern translator has to take liberties with the text! The Welsh hymn, apart from this, has an imaginative nobility.

Erik Routley wrote in 1981:

> I always remember hearing CRUGYBAR on, of all places, Paddington station. I was in the 9.50 for Oxford after a Sunday job in London (this was in the middle 1950s) and the 9.25 for Cardiff was at the adjacent platform; suddenly the strains of CRUGYBAR filled the station, and yes, there was a funeral party joining the Cardiff train, singing most movingly: in a high key (F major) of course, as the Welsh always do. I love the ending of your version.

V

EARLY HYMNS

During his earlier ministry, Fred wrote five hymns which are printed here to make the record complete.

196 The Flame Bearer

8.6.8.6.D.
(D.C.M.)

God lit a flame in Bethlehem,
O Light! O Living Way!
And every saint who held it high
Was faithful in his day.
And now the splendid torch is ours,
For youthful hands to hold,
That fires once lit in Galilee
May light an English wold.

Thus we would consecrate our hands
To the same shining task,
And call Thy Spirit down on us
And for Thy presence ask.
O may no unlit heart be here,
No feet that miss the Way;
O let no cherished hope be lost,
No bright love ember gray.

Lord! fan thine ancient Faith in us,
The bearer of the Flame,
That every thought and deed may be
A hallowing of thy Name;
That in the yet unravelled years
Flamebearers still to be,
Taking the torch from us shall say;
'These Lord, were true to Thee!'

This hymn, Fred's first, was written for the then new Hunmanby Hall School, at which he was Chaplain from 1928 to 1931, for use at the Lamplighting Ceremony on the first day of each term . . . and has continued to be sung (to FOREST GREEN) for over fifty years.

197 Creation

How wonderful this world of Thine,
A fragment of a fiery sun.
How lovely and how small!
Where all things serve Thy great design,
Where life's adventure is begun
In God, the life of all.

The smallest seed in secret grows,
And thrusting upward answers soon
The bidding of the light;
The bud unfurls into a rose;
The wings within the white cocoon
Are perfected for flight.

The migrant bird, in winter fled,
Shall come again with spring and build
In this same shady tree;
By secret wisdom surely led,
Homeward across the clover-field
Hurries the honey-bee.

O Thou, whose greater gifts are ours:
A conscious will, a thinking mind,
A heart to worship Thee—
O take these strange unfolding powers
And teach us through Thy Son to find
The life more full and free.

This early hymn is explained in Fred's 1966 scrapbook:

> Written about 1947, in a garden at Clare, for a tune by Handel which Francis Westbrook, an old college friend, wanted to include in the *School Hymn-Book of the Methodist Church*.

Whilst he has been reluctant to see it used further, others have disagreed and it is included in the Third Edition of the *Church Hymnary*.

198 The Long Ascent

11 10.7 7.9.

Let my vision, Lord, be keen and clear this day;
Clear the air is when mists are blown away;
Show my upward-searching eyes
Sunlit peaks and cloudless skies,
To the summit turn my eyes this day.

Give me courage, Lord, to face the long ascent;
Sense to follow where others safely went;
Give me wisdom, Lord, to read
Map and compass in my need;
Give me comrades for the long ascent.

Free to falter, Lord, we meet the challenge still:
Not for us, Lord, the lounging, laggard will;
Though the mountain hides in mist,
We shall stumble to its crest;
When we reach it, climb a higher still.

Some are starting now and some have gained the height;
All are comrades who keep the end in sight;
All who take you as their guide;
Turn not back, nor turn aside;
They shall stand there on the sunlit height.

This early hymn was written in 1948 for Francis Westbrook's tune ASCENT
to be used in *The School Hymn-Book of the Methodist Church*. No doubt it
was partly inspired by Fred's love of fell-walking in the Lake District. It was
used as the theme song for a school journey by English children to Norway in
1967. Fred's very first scrapbook contains a card signed by all the children
which reads:

> We all have greatly appreciated singing 'Let my vision'. It
> has been so very appropriate. We sung it during our Sunday
> Morning Service in this 11th-Century Stone Church.
> Greetings and good wishes from us all.

The picture included the Garno Church, a Stave Church.

199 Break down the Barriers

S.M.

Father of every race,
Our Ground of Unity,
Be thou the glory of this House
We dedicate to Thee.

Here shall the stranger test
The truth of brotherhood;
Here find in all that alienates
The reconciling good.

O break the barriers down
That keep Thy sons apart
And may this very House declare
That Love is what thou art.

Then let the word be peace
To all who come or go;
And let the Master's will be done—
Better than servants know.

This early hymn was written in 1961 for the opening of Hull International House, of which Fred was one of the founders. Here 50 men of differing age, race, creed, colour and tradition were to live under one roof in harmony and in a friendly atmosphere. In this revised version 'every race' has replaced 'all mankind'. In 1961 no one worried about sexist language!

The tune Fred used—for the first but certainly not the last time—was FRANCONIA.

200 A Christmas Lullaby

7.6 6.7.1.

Sleep, my little King of kings;
Caesars in uneasy sleep
Tremble for their crowns and weep;
Sleep, my little King of kings:
Sleep...

Sleep, my little Lamb of God;
Levites watch with weary eyes
Where the victim bleeds and dies;
Sleep, my little Lamb of God:
Sleep . . .

Sleep, my little Shepherd, sleep;
Shepherds mindful of the wolves,
Count the stars to wake themselves;
Sleep, my little Shepherd, sleep:
Sleep . . .

Sleep, my little Saviour, sleep;
Sinners, helpless to atone,
Toss upon their beds and moan,
Sleep. my little Saviour, sleep:
Sleep . . .

Sleep, my Bright, my Morning Star;
Though the voice of chanticleer
Cries 'The Day of Days is here!'
Sleep, my Bright, my Morning star:
Sleep . . .

This was written at the request of Francis Westbrook who set it to music. It was printed in the *Methodist Recorder* in November, 1962, and sung in Westminster Abbey by Farringtons School Choir in 1971, when it was included in *26 Hymns*. The tune is also called A CHRISTMAS LULLABY.

VI

ANTHEM TEXTS

201 Love is a Mystery

How great a mystery,
Lord, is your love for me;
I scarcely dare believe you walked our human ways.

Jesus of History,
You came to die for me:
Jesus! Jesus! How can I sing your praise?

Love never counts the cost,
Goes to the uttermost:
Love seeks to save us from the judgement we deserve.

You gave yourself for us,
Love is your way with us:
Jesus! Jesus! Save us that we may serve.

Set by Martin Ellis *In the Beauty of Holiness* (Novello)

202 Jesus, Redeemer

Jesus, Redeemer, friend of the friendless,
Give us your courage; give us a quiet spirit.
You by your suffering share our adversity.
When we are tempted, making intercession for us.
Jesus, Redeemer, Man of sorrows,
Friend of the friendless, pray for us sinners.
Yours is the Kingdom, yours the glory:
Help us when living and when dying. Amen.

203 Lord and Master

Lord and Master,
Born to save us,
You have promised
Life indeed:
By your anguish,
By your courage,
By your glory,
Lord, we plead:
May your presence,
Your compassion,
Raise us up,
And meet our need.

Lord and Master,
Born to save us,
Wonderful the names you bear:
Servant, Shepherd,
Friend and brother.
Christ, the Bright, the Morning Star:
King of Glory,
Only Saviour,
Yours we are for evermore.

Set by Martin Ellis *In Wonder, Love & Praise* (Novello, 1978)

204 Love is his Name!

Love is the name he bears;
Love is the robe he wears:
And Love is his silent answer
To our unspoken prayers.

Love is the name he bears;
Love is the Way he prepares:
And Love is his hidden answer,
Buried beneath our cares.

Love is the name he bears;
Love is the life he shares:
And Love is his dying answer,
World, to your despairs.

Love is the Son he sends;
Love is his gift to his friends:
And Love is the deathless Kingdom
To which our life ascends!

Love is God!

Set by Francis Westbrook, *Love is his Name*
(Williams School of Church Music 1974.)

205 Word of Grace

Now the silence, Lord, is broken;
Now I hear your word of grace;
Now my sins are overtaken
By a love I dare not face:
Lest my new-found faith be shaken,
Hold me fast in your embrace.

Lord, defend us in temptation,
Jesus, Captain of salvation,
Unto you be endless praise.

206 Knocking at the Stable Door

The newly-born, they are not always welcome:
A cold wind rocks the cradles of the poor.
Who will comfort them and make them welcome?

How weak and helpless are the little ones:
Fledgling in nest and lion-cub in the lair!
Before legs strengthen or wings take to air,
How weak and helpless are the little ones:

Mary's Son, knocking on the stable-door:
What will they do to him before all is done,
This Saviour, knocking on the stable-door?

207 Hymn of Love

Though I speak with tongues of men and angels,
Though I have the prophet's gift,
Though I hold the key to hidden knowledge,
Though my faith can mountains shift:
Without love I am no better.
Without love it's all for naught:
Lord, you spent your life in loving others:
What this means I would be taught.

Love is kind and patient, knows no envy,
Never gloats when others sin;
Love is never glad to see injustice,
Always wants the truth to win.
There's no end to love's endurance,
There's no test it cannot face;
Lord, you spent your life in loving others:
I shall fail without your grace.

Though there'll be an end to hidden knowledge,
Visions, raptures, prophecy:
Faith and hope and love shall last for ever,
Love the greatest of the three.
Without love I am no better,
Without love it's all for naught;
Lord, you gave your life in saving others:
What this means I would be taught.

This was written for a tune DEVOTION, by the late Edwin Quick, formerly
choirmaster of Westborough Methodist Church, Scarborough, England.

208 Song of the Four Evangelists

We will sing you a song
Of Matthew, Mark, Luke and John.

The sign of Matthew is a Man,
The sign of Mark is a Lion,
The sign of Luke is an Ox,
The sign of John is an Eagle.

Matthew wrote as a Jew,
Mark wrote as a friend of Peter,
Luke wrote as a doctor,
John wrote as an old man thinking things over.

We have Four Gospels,
We might have had only one—or none:
So thanks be to God
For Matthew, Mark, Luke and John.

209 Who comes Riding?

Who comes riding on a donkey's back?
He cannot be an Emperor!
An Emperor rides a war-horse,
He has soldiers to protect him:
Trumpets sound as he enters the city.

Who comes riding on a donkey's back?
He cannot be a Rich Merchant!
A Rich Merchant rides a camel,
He has servants with money-bags:
Beggars pester him as he enters the city.

Who comes riding on a donkey's back?
It is Jesus of Nazareth!
He has not come to conquer us,
Nor to sell us anything
He is coming, He is coming to save the world!
Hosanna! (*shouted*)
Hosanna! (*shouted*)
Blessed is he who comes in the name of the Lord.

Set by Austin Lovelace, *Who comes Riding?* (The Choristers' Guild, USA.)

Acknowledgements

Permission to quote from correspondence is gratefully acknowledged.

A brief extract from *An English Speaking Hymnal Guide* (Erik Routley), is printed by permission of the Liturgical Press, St. John's Abbey, Collegeville, Minnesota 56321, USA, and an extract from *The Hymn* is printed by permission of The Hymn Society of Great Britain and Ireland, 7 Little Cloister, Westminster Abbey, London, SW1P 3PL, England.

The following hymn texts are not controlled by the publishers of this book; thanks is expressed for permission to print. Application for further use should be addressed as follows:

Hymn No.

74	Seaford College, Crosswayte, Lavington Park, Petworth, Sussex, GU28 0NE, England.
84(*)	(For World except USA): SCM Press Ltd., 56–58 Bloomsbury Street, London, WC1B 3QX, England who control *Letters and Papers from Prison*, Dietrich Bonhoeffer (Enlarged Edition) © SCM Press 1971. (For USA): Macmillan Publishing Co. Inc., 866 Third Avenue, New York, NY 10022, USA.
110	The Scout Association, Baden-Powell House, Queen's Gate, London, SW7 5JS, England.
114	The Dean and Chapter of St. Paul's Cathedral, 5 Amen Court, London, EC4M 7BU, England.
115	National Committee for England, Wales and Northern Ireland of Women's World Day of Prayer, Strawberry Lodge, Strawberry Lane, Carshalton, Surrey, SM5 2NQ, England.
123	The Minister, St. Ninian's Priory, Whithorn, Newton Stewart, DG8 8PY, Scotland.
126–146	Mrs. Louise Bristol, 7 Armour Road, Princeton, New Jersey 08540, USA. The following items (together with 85 and 159 controlled by the Publishers) are being published in 1982 with settings by the late Lee Hastings Bristol, Jnr under the title of *May We Have a Word With You*: 126, 128, 130, 132, 133, 134, 135, 136, 137, 138, 139, 140, 141.
175	Hänssler-Verlag, Postfach 1220, Neuhausen-Stuttgart, Germany.
184(*)	(For World except USA): SCM Press Ltd., 56–58 Bloomsbury Street, London, WC1B 3QX, England. (For USA): Macmillan Publishing Co. Inc., 866 Third Avenue, New York, NY 10022, USA.
(*)	For these hymns permission is also needed from Stainer & Bell Ltd. (for the World except USA and Canada) and from Hope Publishing Company (for the USA and Canada).

For permission to make copies locally or otherwise, on all other texts, application should be made to: Stainer & Bell Ltd. (World except USA and Canada), 82 High Road, London, N2 9PW, England. Hope Publishing Company (USA and Canada), Carol Stream, Illinois 60187, USA.

Bibliography

32 Galliard Carols for Christmas Stainer & Bell Ltd., 82 High Road, London, N2 9PW, England. (For USA: Galaxy Music Corporation, 131 West 86th Street, New York, NY 10024.)

26 Hymns Methodist Publishing House, Wellington Road, London, SW19, England.

A.D. Magazine A.D. Publications Inc., General Offices, 475 Riverside Drive, New York, NY 10027, USA.

American Lutheran Hymnal Concordia Publishing Company, 3558 So. Jefferson Avenue, St. Louis, Missouri 63118, USA.

Australian Hymn-Book William Collins Publishers Pty Ltd., Box 476, G.P.O. Sydney 2001, Australia.

Boys' Brigade Hymn-Book Brigade House, Parsons Green, London, SW6, England.

Broadcast Praise Oxford University Press, Ely House, 37 Dover Street, London, W1, England.

Cambridge Hymnal Cambridge University Press, The Pitt Building, Trumpington Street, Cambridge, CB2 8BA, England.

Canadian Catholic Hymnal Gordon V. Thompson Ltd., 29 Birch Avenue, Toronto, M4V 1E2, Canada.

Canadian Hymn-Book Offices of the Synod, Anglican Church of Canada, 600 Jarvis Street, Toronto, Ontario, M4Y 2J6, Canada.

Cantate Domino Oxford University Press, Ely House, 37 Dover Street, London, W1, England.

Church Hymnary Oxford University Press, Ely House, 37 Dover Street, London, W1, England.

Early English Church Music Stainer & Bell Ltd., 82 High Road, London, N2 9PW, England.

Ecumenical Praise Agape (Hope Publishing Company), Carol Stream, Illinois 60187, USA.

English Hymnal Oxford University Press, Ely House, 37 Dover Street, London, W1, England.

English Praise Oxford University Press, Ely House, 37 Dover Street, London, W1, England.

English Speaking Hymnal Guide, An Liturgical Press, St. John's Abbey, Collegeville, Minnesota 56321, USA.

Expository Times T. & T. Clark Ltd., 36 George Street, Edinburgh, EH2 2LQ, Scotland.

Galliard Book of Carols, The Stainer & Bell Ltd., 82 High Road, London, N2 9PW, England. (For USA: Barnes & Noble Books, Biblio Distribution Centre, 81 Adams Drive, PO Box 327, Totowa, New Jersey 07511.)

Hymn, The Hymn Society of America, Wittenberg University, Springfield, Ohio 45501, USA.

Hymns Ancient and Modern Revised Hymns Ancient and Modern Ltd., 16 Commerce Way, Colchester, Essex, CO2 8HH, England.

Hymns and Songs Methodist Publishing House, Wellington Road, London, SW19, England.

Hymns for Celebration Royal School of Church Music, Addington Palace, Croydon, Surrey, England.

Hymns for the Homeless   Shelter National Campaign for the Homeless Ltd., 157 Waterloo Road, London, SE1, England.

Hymns of the Saints   Herald Publishing House, Independence, Missouri 64055, USA.

Hymn-Book of the Church of England in Canada   Offices of the Synod, Anglican Church of Canada, 600 Jarvis Street, Toronto, Ontario, M4Y 2J6, Canada.

Hymns of Faith and Life   Light and Life Press, Winoa Lake, Indiana 46590, USA.

In the Beauty of Holiness   Novello & Co. Ltd., Fairfield Road, Borough Green, Sevenoaks, Kent, England.

In Wonder, Love and Praise   Novello & Co. Ltd., Fairfield Road, Borough Green, Sevenoaks, Kent, England.

Jesus Christ frees and unites   World Council of Churches, Publications Office, PO Box 66, 150 Route de Ferney, 1211 Geneva 20, Switzerland.

Johannine Hymnal   American Catholic Press, 1223 Rossell Avenue, Oak Park, Illinois 60302, USA.

Loose-Leaf Book of the Episcopal Church in America (*The Hymnal 1940*)   The Church Hymnal Corporation, 800 Second Avenue, New York, NY 10017, USA.

Lutheran Book of Worship   Augsberg Publishing House, 426 South Fifth Street, Minneapolis, Minnesota 55415, USA.

The Marriage Service with Music   Royal School of Church Music, Addington Palace, Croydon, Surrey, England.

Methodist Recorder   176 Fleet Street, London, EC4, England.

More Hymns for Today   Hymns Ancient and Modern Ltd., 16 Commerce Way, Colchester, Essex, CO2 8HH, England.

New Church Praise   Saint Andrew Press, 121 George Street, Edinburgh, EH2 4YN, Scotland.

One World Songs   Department of Social Responsibility of the Methodist Church, Westminster Central Hall, London, SW1, England.

Oxford Book of Carols   Oxford University Press, Ely House, 37 Dover Street, London, W1, England.

Partners in Praise   Stainer & Bell Ltd., 82 High Road, London, N2 9PW, England. (For USA: Abingdon Press, 201 Eighth Avenue South, Nashville, Tennessee 37202.)

Penguin Book of Christmas Carols   Penguin Books Ltd., Bath Road, Harmondsworth, West Drayton, Middlesex, UB7 0DA, England.

Pilgrim Praise   Stainer & Bell Ltd., 82 High Road, London, N2 9PW, England. (For USA: Galaxy Music Corporation, 131 West 86th Street, New York, NY 10024.)

Pocket Praise   British Council of Churches Youth Unit, 2 Eaton Gate, London, SW1W 9BL, England.

Praise for Today   Baptist Union of Great Britain and Ireland, 4 Southampton Row, London, WC1, England.

Praise the Lord   Geoffrey Chapman Ltd., 35 Red Lion Square, London, WC1R 4SG, England.

Praiseways   The Presbyterian Church in Canada, 50 Wynford Drive, Don Mills, Ontario, M3C 1J7, Canada.

Revised Hymnal of the Southern Baptists   Convention Press, Baptist Sunday School Board, 127 Ninth Avenue, No., Nashville, Tennessee 37203, USA.

Risk   (Nairobi Assembly Edition), World Council of Churches, Publications Office, PO Box 66, 150 Route de Ferney, 1211 Geneva 20, Switzerland.

St. Deiniol Carol Book   Bangor Diocesan Office, Gwynedd Road, Bangor, Gwynedd, Wales.

School Hymn-Book of the Methodist Church   Methodist Division of Education and Youth, 2 Chester House, Pages Lane, London, N10, England.

Sing New Songs   National Christian Education Council, Robert Denholm House, Nutfield, Redhill, Surrey, England.

Sixteen Hymns of Today   Royal School of Church Music, Addington Palace, Croydon, Surrey, England.

Sixteen New Hymns on the Stewardship of the Environment   Hymn Society of America, Wittenberg University, Springfield, Ohio 45501, USA.

Songs of Celebration   World Council of Churches, Publications Office, PO Box 66, 150 Route de Ferney, 1211 Geneva 20, Switzerland.

Songs of Praise   Oxford University Press, Ely House, 37 Dover Street, London, W1, England.

Songs of Thanks and Praise   Hinshaw Music Inc., P.O. Box 470, Chapel Hill, North Carolina 27514, USA.

Songs for the Seventies   Stainer & Bell Ltd., 82 High Road, London, N2 9PW, England.

Songs for Worship   Scripture Union, 5 Wigmore Street, London, W1H 0AD, England.

Sounds of Salvation (recording)   Home Mission Division of the Methodist Church, 1 Central Buildings, Westminster, London, SW1H 9NH, England.

Together for Festivals   Church Information Office, Church House, Deans Yard, London, SW1, England.

Thirty-two Galliard Carols for Christmas   Stainer & Bell Ltd., 82 High Road, London, N2 9PW, England. (For USA: Galaxy Music Corporation, 131 West 86th Street, New York, NY 10024.)

Twenty-six Hymns   Methodist Publishing House, Wellington Road, London, SW19, England.

Westminster Praise   Hinshaw Music Inc., PO Box 470, Chapel Hill, North Carolina 27514, USA.

Worship II   G.I.A. Publications Inc., 7404 So. Mason Avenue, Chicago, Illinois 60638, USA.

The address of The Williams School of Church Music is: The Bourne, 20 Salisbury Avenue, Harpenden, Hertfordshire, AL5 2QG, England.

Subject Index

GOD

The Trinity
Christ is the world's Light, he and none other   *2*
Rejoice with us in God, the Trinity   *15*

God: the Creator
For the fruits of his creation   *20*
Let us praise Creation's Lord   *93*
Life has no mystery as great   *45*
Lord, you do not need our praises   *28*
We come to worship you, O Lord, whose glory is so great   *74*
We look into your heavens and see   *46*

God: His Love
God saw that it was good   *73*
Lord, I repent my sin   *89*
One God and Father of us all!   *56*
One in Christ, we meet together   *40*
Other gospel there is none   *14*
Rejoice with us in God, the Trinity   *15*

God: His Purpose and Providence
All who worship God in Jesus, all who serve the Son of Man   *43*
God in his love for us lent us this planet   *21*
God is here! As we his people   *76*
It is God who holds the nations in the hollow of his hand   *72*
Lord God, in whom all worlds   *91*
Now praise the hidden God of Love   *58*
Sing to the Lord a new song, for he does wonders   *175*
The God who sent the prophets   *88*
When our confidence is shaken   *29*

God: His Kingdom
All who worship God in Jesus, all who serve the Son of Man   *43*
God is here! As we his people   *76*
Lord God, when we complain   *53*
Lord, you do not need our praises   *28*
Other gospel there is none   *14*
What is our earth but a prison   *192*
What joy it is to worship here   *90*
When Jesus came preaching the kingdom of God   *158*
Where Christ is, his Church is there   *27*

God: His Word
The Church of Christ in every age   *10*

(*cont.*)

JESUS CHRIST

244

245

THE HOLY SPIRIT

THE CHURCH

Christian Unity
(See Jesus Christ, Unity in Christ)

THE CHRISTIAN LIFE

248

249

250

251

SPECIAL OCCASIONS

BIBLICAL AND OTHER CHARACTERS

253

The Church, in Advent, from of old   *95*
The Word is born this very night   *31*
This is the night of his coming to earth   *50*

Who anointed him
Praise her, as Jesus did!   *130*

Who gave all
Where Temple offerings are made   *129*

Woman who touched him
One woman none could heal   *127*

Zacchaeus
Zacchaeus in the pay of Rome   *137*

Index of Scripture Texts

These passages have either inspired or support the hymn texts.

Chapter	*Hymn*	*Chapter*	*Hymn*

<table>
<tr><td colspan="2" align="center">PSALMS</td><td colspan="2" align="center">MICAH</td></tr>
<tr><td>5, 3</td><td>48</td><td>6, 6–8</td><td>15</td></tr>
<tr><td>19</td><td>46</td><td>6, 8</td><td>158</td></tr>
<tr><td>23</td><td>58</td><td></td><td></td></tr>
<tr><td>23, 1</td><td>38</td><td></td><td></td></tr>
<tr><td>24, 1</td><td>21</td><td colspan="2" align="center">MATTHEW</td></tr>
<tr><td>67</td><td>72</td><td></td><td></td></tr>
<tr><td>72, 12–13</td><td>10</td><td>2, 1–12</td><td>150</td></tr>
<tr><td>84, 1–2</td><td>38</td><td>2, 13–18</td><td>63</td></tr>
<tr><td>96</td><td>54, 175</td><td>2, 19–23</td><td>153</td></tr>
<tr><td>102, 1–7</td><td>6</td><td>3, 13–17</td><td>24</td></tr>
<tr><td>118, 14</td><td>54</td><td>4, 1–11</td><td>102, 154</td></tr>
<tr><td>137</td><td>82</td><td>4, 4</td><td>30</td></tr>
<tr><td>139</td><td>194</td><td>5, 9</td><td>79</td></tr>
<tr><td>150</td><td>39, 93</td><td>5, 10</td><td>83</td></tr>
<tr><td></td><td></td><td>5, 23–24</td><td>49</td></tr>
<tr><td></td><td></td><td>5, 48</td><td>15</td></tr>
<tr><td colspan="2" align="center">ISAIAH</td><td>6, 1–6</td><td>19</td></tr>
<tr><td></td><td></td><td>6, 17–18</td><td>140</td></tr>
<tr><td>1, 4–9</td><td>21</td><td>6, 28–34</td><td>112, 113</td></tr>
<tr><td>1, 9</td><td>88</td><td>7, 7</td><td>5</td></tr>
<tr><td>6, 1–8</td><td>9</td><td>9, 14–17</td><td>140</td></tr>
<tr><td>10, 20–22</td><td>88</td><td>9, 17</td><td>42</td></tr>
<tr><td>11</td><td>17</td><td>10, 37–39</td><td>103</td></tr>
<tr><td>11, 1–9</td><td>95</td><td>11, 28–30</td><td>69</td></tr>
<tr><td>27, 13</td><td>50</td><td>13, 33</td><td>158</td></tr>
<tr><td>40, 12–26</td><td>72</td><td>16, 24</td><td>190</td></tr>
<tr><td>41, 1</td><td>35</td><td>17, 20</td><td>101</td></tr>
<tr><td>42, 1–4</td><td>10</td><td>17, 21</td><td>140</td></tr>
<tr><td>53</td><td>88</td><td>18, 20</td><td>27, 80</td></tr>
<tr><td>61, 1</td><td>82</td><td>18, 22</td><td>42</td></tr>
<tr><td></td><td></td><td>19, 13–15</td><td>26</td></tr>
<tr><td></td><td></td><td>19, 16–22</td><td>134</td></tr>
<tr><td></td><td></td><td>20, 1–16</td><td>20</td></tr>
<tr><td colspan="2" align="center">JEREMIAH</td><td>20, 20–28</td><td>157</td></tr>
<tr><td></td><td></td><td>21, 6–11</td><td>64</td></tr>
<tr><td>1, 4–9</td><td>9</td><td>21, 10–13</td><td>4</td></tr>
<tr><td></td><td></td><td>24, 44</td><td>163</td></tr>
<tr><td></td><td></td><td>25, 10</td><td>163</td></tr>
<tr><td></td><td></td><td>25, 34</td><td>27, 43</td></tr>
<tr><td colspan="2" align="center">LAMENTATIONS</td><td>25, 37–45</td><td>20</td></tr>
<tr><td></td><td></td><td>26, 31–35</td><td>157</td></tr>
<tr><td>3, 22–23</td><td>48</td><td>26, 36–46</td><td>4</td></tr>
<tr><td></td><td></td><td>26, 56</td><td>157</td></tr>
<tr><td></td><td></td><td>27, 27–32</td><td>19, 32</td></tr>
<tr><td colspan="2" align="center">AMOS</td><td>27, 27–35</td><td>67</td></tr>
<tr><td></td><td></td><td>27, 45</td><td>4</td></tr>
<tr><td>6, 1–7</td><td>6</td><td>28, 19–20</td><td>10</td></tr>
</table>

257

Chapter	Hymn	Chapter	Hymn
10, 10	5	5	89
11, 50	43	5, 5	79
12, 20–22	149	5, 6–9	4
12, 35–36	18	5, 6–11	73
13, 1–17	33	5, 8	29
14, 1–2	35	5, 14–18	16
14, 1–3	33, 59	6, 15–19	3
14, 6	77	8, 15	24
14, 8–10	2	8, 22–24	102
14, 16	24	8, 31–39	37
15, 14–16	71	8, 35	70
16, 13	12	8, 35–39	23
17, 20–26	2, 15	12, 6	1
18, 28–40	138		
19, 1–16	138		
19, 25–27	51		
19, 39	159		
20	86		
20, 11–18	131		
21, 15	163		
21, 15–17	12, 66, 85		

1 CORINTHIANS

1, 10–11	14, 15, 49
1, 12–13	118
2, 8	77
3, 3–4	14, 15
3, 9	91
7, 5	191
8, 6	56
9, 24–27	111

ACTS

1, 1–11	96	10, 26	21, 48
1, 1–14	143	11, 18–19	14, 15, 49
1, 9–11	3	12, 4–11	100
2, 1–4	12, 96	12, 12–26	182
2, 1–13	143	12, 27–31	76
2, 46	8	13,	13, 207
4, 12	42	13, 1	93
5, 32	12	13, 5	23
8, 26–40	145	13, 12	59
9, 1–30	144	15, 20	35
10	145	15, 20–28	177
10, 44	143	15, 25	2
14, 14–17	21	15, 57	5
16, 15	25	15, 57–58	177
27, 41–44	145		

2 CORINTHIANS

2, 14	193
3, 14	30
3, 17	8, 79

ROMANS

1, 18–32	149	4, 5	76
1, 28–32	6	4, 6	93
		5, 14–17	45
		5, 18–19	4

Index of first lines

(in alphabetical order, including first lines of choruses)

261

Infant in the stall, all our sins destroy! 99
In that land which we call Holy *19*
It is God who holds the nations in the hollow of his hand *72*
It may be they were Magi *150*
It shocked them that the Master did not fast *140*
It was fair weather when we set sail *155*
It was Jesus who said we must persevere *162*

Jesus Christ, for forty days *154*
Jesus, how strong is our desire *193*
Jesus is God's gift to us *107*
Jesus is the Lord of Glory 77
Jesus in the olive grove *4*
Jesus, Redeemer, friend of the friendless *202*

Let every Christian pray *12*
Let my vision, Lord, be keen and clear this day *198*
Let us all praise him *110*
Let us praise Creation's Lord *93*
Let us rejoice in Christ *64*
Life has many rhythms, every heart its beat *5*
Life has no mystery as great *45*
Little children, welcome! *26*
Lo! God's Son is now ascended *96*
Long ago, prophets knew *17*
Look! the sun awakes the sky *68*
Lord and Master *203*
Lord, do you trust yourself to me? *103*
Lord God, in whom all worlds *91*
Lord God, when we complain *53*
Lord, I repent my sin *89*
Lord Jesus, once a child *25*
Lord Jesus, you were homeless *142*
Lord, let us listen when you speak! *182*
Lord, now it's time to pray *47*
Lord of every art and science *57*
Lord, we have come at your own invitation *71*
Lord, when you singled out the Three *66*
Lord, you are at many tables *181*

Lord, you do not need our praises *28*
Lo! Today into our world the Word is born *174*
Love is the name he bears *204*
Loving Lord, as now we gather *75*

Man cannot live on bread alone *30*
Mary sang to her Son: Don't you cry, little one! *156*
Men go to God when they are in despair *84*

262

263

Index of Tunes

Many of the tunes are well-known and printed in a wide range of hymn books. Others are published alongside the texts of Fred Pratt Green in the various publications mentioned in the text, about which further details are given in the Bibliography.

Where a tune is followed by (x) in the index it is as yet unpublished and held in a Tunes Bank maintained by the Publishers. Copies can be supplied on payment of a small fee if application is made to Hope Publishing Company, Carol Stream, Illinois 60187 for the USA and Canada or to Stainer & Bell Limited, 82 High Road, London N2 9PW, for the rest of the world.

For unpublished tunes noted by other codes after the tune name, contact should be made as follows:

(a) Mr. Michael Dawney, 5 Queen's Road, Parkstone, Poole, Dorset, BH14 9HF, England.
(b) Mrs. Louise Bristol, 7 Armour Road, Princeton, New Jersey 08540, USA.
(c) Mr. Hubert Julian, Little Home Parc, Kenwyn, Truro, Cornwall, England.
(d) Oxford University Press, Ely House, 37 Dover Street, London, W1, England.
(e) Mr. Ewart Knight, 3 Barton Court, The Triangle, Sidmouth, Devon, EX10 8PJ, England.
(f) Dr. Francis Jackson, Nethergarth, Acklam, Malton, North Yorkshire, England.

For the unnamed tunes by Mr. Lee Hastings Bristol, Junr, mentioned in the text, contact should be made with Mrs. Louise Bristol (see (b) above). The Publishers will do what they can to assist if difficulties arise in tracking down copies of any tune.